Managing the Devolved Budget

Second Edition

Essential skills for The public sector

HB PUBLICATIONS

Jennifer Bean
Lascelles Hussey

HB PUBLICATIONS
(Incorporated as Givegood Limited)

Published by:

**HB Publications
London, England**

First Published 1996 © HB Publications
Second Edition 2011 © HB Publications

British Library Cataloguing in Publication Data

ISBN 978-1-899448-72-2

For further information see www.hbpublications.com
and www.fci-system.com

Contents

Chapter 1

Introduction

The control of public finances is always a key issue for scrutiny by Government. With increasing pressure on resources and increasing demand for public services, good financial management is essential. In response, the public sector has had to take a positive approach to implementing successful systems for financial management and control. Devolving budgets to individuals, making them responsible and accountable, has become a commonly adopted method for achieving the effective control of financial resources, and obtaining value for money. This is often a new area of activity and requires them to have a certain level of financial skill.

Managing the Devolved Budget has been developed to meet the needs of those working in public sector environments such as central government; local and regional authorities; health authorities; police authorities; educational institutions, and so on. The text is particularly relevant as many public sector employees have now been given some form of budgetary responsibility.

The publication has been designed to be used for reference and act as an important part of a managers own personal development. At the conclusion of each chapter is a series of exercises which encourage the reader to focus on the key issues covered. Suggested solutions to the exercises are provided in the final section.

Managing The Devolved Budget is presented in a simple format which is easy to read and makes practical sense. It will give those who have any form of budgetary responsibility an understanding of the process behind budget setting and control, and will provide tools with which they can undertake these tasks with greater awareness and confidence.

It is recognised that many budget holders work within constraints. This may be with respect to policies, limited resources, limited support, and restricted access to financial experts. Although circumstances may not be perfect, ideas are given within the text which will enable the most common constraints to be taken into account whilst allowing the budget holder to achieve the objective of controlling a budget.

The task of financial management and control is now relevant to many job descriptions in the public sector. For those who may wish to pursue a career within public service, this book will highlight the type of knowledge and skill now required to be fully prepared for acquiring budgetary responsibilities.

This book is one of a series of "Essential Skills for the Public Sector" titles. The series aims to assist public sector managers become more efficient and effective in carrying out their important management responsibilities. We consider this book to be an important part of the tool kit for public sector management development.

Chapter 2

Devolving the Budget

What is Devolvement?

It is necessary to firstly clarify the meaning of devolvement as this term carries many interpretations and definitions. For the purpose of this text, the following definition should be used.

Devolvement is:

> ***the process whereby budgets are devolved to an individual who becomes the budget holder and who will be totally responsible and accountable for that budget. Ideally management and financial responsibilities are aligned such that the budget holder is accountable for the financial implications of his/her management decisions.***

Other terms that are often used interchangeably with devolvement are "delegation" and "decentralisation". Both these activities usually take place as part of the process of devolvement. Usually budgets are firstly decentralised, then devolved, and then sometimes delegated. In order to understand these terms more clearly, the definitions of delegation and decentralisation for the purpose of this text are given below:

Decentralisation is:

> ***where the control of budgets is dis-aggregated from the centre and allocated to other areas of the organisation such as departments, divisions, branches etc.***

Delegation is:

> ***where budgets are delegated to nominated budget holders who are responsible for <u>monitoring</u> the budget, but are not accountable for the budget as they will have little or no control over its construction and its usage.***

There are some common factors that apply to all three terms:

- *They all involve a transfer of financial control to some degree away from a central point*
- *They all result in finance being more closely linked to service delivery or activity*
- *They all result in a spreading of financial responsibilities throughout the organisation*

In order to further appreciate the difference between each of the three terms, it is helpful to illustrate the normal devolvement process by way of the following chart:

DEVOLVEMENT IN A LOCAL AUTHORITY

LOCAL AUTHORITY SPENDING COMMITTEE

CENTRAL FINANCE DEPARTMENT

Has control of all budgets. Approves all expenditure. Decides on resource allocation between departments.

↓ 1st Stage Decentralisation

SERVICE DEPARTMENTS

e.g. Housing Services

Has own budget and usually own finance department. Budgets across all aspects of service aggregated. Approval of expenditure and resource allocation taken by senior management

↓ 1st Stage Devolvement

SERVICE DIVISIONS

e.g. Housing Management

Service division heads given responsibility for their service budgets. They approve expenditure and make decisions on resource allocation.

↓ 2nd Stage Devolvement

SERVICE MANAGERS

e.g. Head of Housing Management

Service managers are given responsibility for management and financial decisions with respect to their area of service. They have autonomy to make and approve expenditure decisions.

↓ Delegation – sometimes leading to 3rd Stage Devolvement

FRONT LINE MANAGERS

e.g. Repairs and Maintenance Manager

Front line managers are given responsibility for monitoring a budget. They are then given full devolvement responsibilities whereby management and financial decisions are aligned.

↓ Delegation

FRONT LINE STAFF

e.g. Repairs Officer

Front line staff given responsibility for monitoring certain aspects of a budget

Why Devolve Budgets?

There are a number of advantages to be gained from devolving a budget, some of which are summarised as follows:

- *Managers and officers who are involved with the direct delivery of a service understand service requirements, and are therefore in the best position to target financial resources efficiently and effectively to the benefit of the end user.*
- *There is greater incentive for budget holders to maximise value for money if they consider they have real control over financial resources, and can reap benefits from the efficient and effective use of the budget.*
- *More effective budget monitoring and control is often achieved as a result of a wider range of people being involved in the budgetary process.*
- *Decisions can be made more quickly if the budget holder responsible for the service can also authorise the use of resources. The budget holder is in a position to exploit opportunities and avoid problems by being in control of the budget.*
- *The budget holder can be held accountable for their decisions, and made to take responsibility for their actions. The impact of management decisions on financial resources can be effectively measured and assessed.*

There are also a number of dis-advantages that need to be taken into account when embarking on a devolvement strategy. These include:

- *Devolvement often requires the person who becomes the budget holder to undertake additional duties including budget monitoring and control activities. These areas may not be part of the individual's job description and will often be an area for which no prior training has been given. Certain budget holders neither have the skill or aptitude for this new task and no desire to acquire it.*

- *Devolvement requires the organisation to give more autonomy to staff lower down the hierarchy, and hence removes some control away from senior management. This may leave senior managers feeling vulnerable if they lack confidence in less senior staff.*

- *Devolvement means that the managers who become budget holders have to take account of the financial consequences of their decisions. This may lead to a conflict of interest in making what would be a "professionally correct" decision, but not necessarily a "financially viable" one.*

Most of the dis-advantages of devolvement may be overcome by undertaking the following activities as part of the devolvement process:

- *Ensuring staff gain a thorough understanding of the meaning and process of devolvement and what their budgetary responsibilities will be in advance of them receiving devolved responsibility.*

- *Ensuring the organisation has established clear guidelines with respect to how devolvement is expected to work. This is achieved by stating where the budget holder's responsibilities begin and end.*

- *Ensuring clear service objectives, priorities, and guidelines, are set such that the budget holder knows how to balance professionalism with respect to service delivery and the new financial responsibilities they hold.*

- *Establishing clarity with respect to budgetary responsibility by appointing one budget holder for each budget. This will ensure there is no misunderstanding with respect to who is responsible for what.*

- *Ensuring budget holders receive sufficient support from senior managers and finance officers, to enable them to undertake their role in an effective and efficient manner for the benefit of the whole organisation.*

Making managers more responsible and accountable for their decisions in financial terms has its benefits; however, achieving the benefit will be dependent on taking a practical approach to devolvement. Devolvement should only occur when due consideration has been given to a range of factors such as the size of budget and the type of budget to be devolved.

The Devolvement Process

The steps in the process may be summarised as follows:

- *Decentralise*
- *Identify appropriate budgets for devolvement*
- *Identify potential budget holders*
- *Provide training and support for budget holders*
- *Ensure budget holders are aware of the service objectives to be achieved with the devolved budgets*
- *Ensure budget holders have the appropriate resources needed to monitor and control budgets, including access to information, Information Technology (IT), administrative staff, and so on*
- *Provide budget holders with real autonomy and flexibility to make decisions with respect to expenditure and service delivery*

Commonly Devolved Budgets

Some of the most commonly devolved budgets are highlighted on the next pages:

Salaries

This budget is one of the most contentious budgets when it comes to devolvement. Salaries tend to be the largest revenue expenditure budget for most public sector organisations, normally representing over half of overall spending. Hence, devolvement to an appropriate level may assist with control and monitoring of this important budget. Depending on the nature of the organisation and service being provided, the appropriate level of devolvement can vary from the most senior person in the hierarchy such as the Chief Executive Officer, to a frontline manager, such as the head of a day nursery.

Supplies and Services

This heading covers a whole range of different budgets. It relates to the expenditure on any item which is used to deliver the service. This may include items such as materials, stationery, and services provided by third parties. These budgets are the most obvious to devolve as they often require decision making on a day to day basis by operational staff.

Property costs

These costs include everything required to run and maintain the property. They include items such as rent, rates, insurance, heat, light, repairs, maintenance, and so on. It is quite usual to devolve these areas of cost to either service managers or a service department. There may be a limit as to how much positive action the budget holder can take with respect to controlling these costs, as some are uncontrollable. For example, rent and rates are normally fixed amounts in the short term and have to be paid. However, in the longer term a devolved budget holder may be in a position to decide on the type and the amount of accommodation required to deliver the service, and therefore have some impact on these costs.

Internal support service costs

In many large organisations, certain activities are performed by centralised departments, or by sections within a department. These activities, which typically include finance, personnel, property (in some cases), information technology, and so on, support the organisation in the delivery of its services. They are essential activities and it is often considered that decentralisation of these types of services should only occur to the extent that economies of scale are not totally lost. It has been common practice to allocate the cost of supporting services to those areas of the organisation that are involved in direct service delivery. This enables the true cost of service delivery to be established.

When budgets for support services are devolved to service managers, they sometimes have little real control over the expenditure. This is because the support service budgets are often allocated on an arbitrary basis, i.e. not linked to usage, and remain fixed for the year. For example, a typical allocation of personnel services may be based on numbers of staff not on the amount of personnel service used by the budget holder. Devolved budgets for support services are only controllable if an internal market exists, and budget holders have the power to decide on the quality or quantity of service that is required.

Capital Expenditure

Capital expenditure represents expenditure on items that have an on-going value to the organisation. These items are often referred to as "fixed assets" in accounting terms, and include land, buildings, furniture, fixtures, fittings, equipment, and so on. The sort of budget that tends to be devolved in this area is the purchase of furniture and equipment which can be easily controlled by the budget holder. Major works projects, such as building work, are often handled by a specialist (and sometimes central) department.

Income

Where a service generates income from fees or charges, the responsibility for controlling the income may readily be devolved to operational staff. An example would be in the case of a leisure centre where entrance and membership fees are charged for a range of different activities. The centre manager would have devolved responsibility to ensure that fee income meets the budgeted income targets.

Level of Devolvement

A school of thought exists which argues that budgets should be devolved to the lowest possible tier within an organisation. This allows the control of spending to be as near to the direct provision of services as possible. For example, in a hospital, certain operational budgets could be devolved to the **ward sister**, or, in a school to a **teacher**, and so on. Devolvement should ideally be to the staff member who makes the spending decision and authorises the expenditure.

Common sense dictates that at certain levels devolvement may become inefficient and difficult to operate. It is therefore necessary to consider the following factors when deciding on an appropriate level of devolvement:

- *Size of organisation*
- *Type of structure*
- *Type of budget*
- *Controllability of budget*
- *Size of budget*

These issues are discussed in the following paragraphs.

Size of Organisation

The size of organisation is very important to the level of devolvement. Larger organisations often require a greater level of devolvement to ensure financial monitoring and control is more closely aligned with the point of service delivery. For example, the budget for materials may be devolved to heads of departments or below in a large further education college, whereas it may not be devolved below the head teacher in a small primary school.

Type of Structure

The organisational structure very often dictates where decisions are made. Usually a public sector organisation has a clear hierarchical structure where key decisions, particularly financial ones, are often taken at the top of the hierarchy. The more levels within the hierarchy, the greater the number of stages in the devolvement process. In a very hierarchical structure, devolvement may not go down to the same level as it would within an organisation with a flatter structure and fewer management tiers.

Type of Budget

The type of budget has an impact on devolvement. For example, a budget for travel expenses may be devolved down to officer level, whereas a budget for property costs may only be devolved to cost centre level. This is because it is not always practical to divide shared overheads, such as property costs, between individuals. In contrast, budgets for items such as travel expenses can be easily identified and devolved to an individual officer for control.

Controllability of Budget

Some budgets are uncontrollable. For example, both central and local government will have statutory responsibilities that have to be met, such as spending in respect to homelessness, healthcare, child protection, and public safety issues. Such service areas have to be provided irrespective of the budget allocation. This makes the budget difficult to control in the short to medium term, and may require changes in legislation in order to modify the statutory requirements.

Size of Budget

Devolving a budget below a certain level can become unworkable depending on the amounts concerned. For example, to devolve a small furniture budget too low, i.e. to each individual member of staff, may lead to the amounts being devolved being insufficient to buy any furniture. These budgets should be held at a level that is practical, in this case, where the budget is of a size that is large enough to meet the furniture purchasing requirements of the service. This may require the budget to be held at a service manager level of even at a departmental level depending to on the furniture requirements.

Being Responsible for a Devolved Budget

A budget holder should be responsible for all aspects of the budget. This includes setting, monitoring and controlling the budget. In order to be effective in this role, the budget holder has to:

- *Become involved with setting the budget in the first instance (although this may not always be possible in the first year of devolvement)*

- *Be given a certain amount of autonomy to make financial decisions and to amend budgets part way through the year as required*

- *Take responsibility if things do not go according to plan*

- *Have support to make decisions through an effective financial and management information system*

The following chapters in the book will help prepare the budget holder to be as effective as possible in their role.

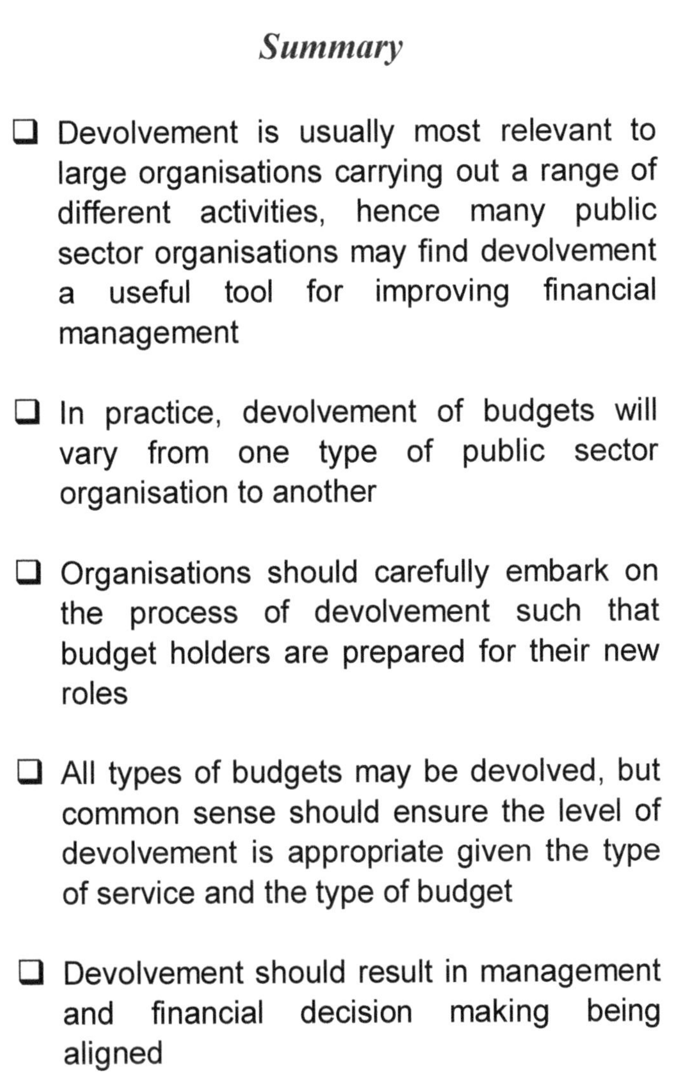

Summary

- Devolvement is usually most relevant to large organisations carrying out a range of different activities, hence many public sector organisations may find devolvement a useful tool for improving financial management

- In practice, devolvement of budgets will vary from one type of public sector organisation to another

- Organisations should carefully embark on the process of devolvement such that budget holders are prepared for their new roles

- All types of budgets may be devolved, but common sense should ensure the level of devolvement is appropriate given the type of service and the type of budget

- Devolvement should result in management and financial decision making being aligned

Exercise 1

Devolvement in Practice

You are given the following scenario:

Blackstone Leisure Centre (BLC) has recently been subject to competitive tendering. Three of the Centre's existing managers decided to come together independently and put in a private bid for BLC, in which they were successful. Having won the tender they now wish to implement devolved budgetary responsibility. Having attended a number of finance courses they are now confused as to how to go about the process. The current situation is described as follows:

The three managers who came together to bid for BLC were the Head of Activities, the Head of Finance and the Head of Repairs, Maintenance and Operations. They have now taken different roles as Centre Director and two Centre Managers and new personnel were appointed to their old posts. Their new responsibilities involve overall responsibility for BLC. Due to the long opening hours it is necessary for shift working and they wish to ensure there is always a Centre Manager on site. There are a total of four areas of operation; these are called service areas, each of which has a Head. The service areas are as follows:

Activities
This includes all the activities that BLC provide such as swimming pool activities, gymnasium activities, fitness classes, sports hall activities, health and beauty treatments and other ad hoc activities as demanded by the public. There are a number of key personnel which include the head swimming pool attendant, the head fitness instructor and a health and safety officer. There are 12 other permanent staff and a large number of

sessional staff used for specific classes/sessions. All staff are appropriately qualified for their jobs.

Finance and Resources
This includes all finance functions, personnel functions and administration. There is a financial controller who is responsible for the day to day bookkeeping, production of reports, payroll etc. who is supported by three other staff. There is a personnel officer responsible for training, as well as all the personnel functions. This officer is supported by one assistant. In addition, there is a senior administrator who currently undertakes all the ordering of goods and services and manages two secretarial staff.

Repairs, Maintenance and Operations
This includes responsibility for all maintenance works within the building, including controlling the maintenance contracts that have been agreed for the boiler systems etc. In addition, this service area is responsible for the cleaning, reception area, external areas such as the car park, and the security. There are 15 to 25 full and part-time staff engaged in this work. Key staff include the contracts officer and the cleaning service manager.

Entertainment
This includes the provision of bar and restaurant facilities, (two main areas in the building) lettings of space to the public for weddings etc., and the arrangement of a number of events during the year, often with a view to promoting BLC. The head of entertainment is also responsible for the general marketing of the Centre including the production of brochures, press releases and so on. There are two full time staff who have key roles, these are the catering manager and the press and publicity officer. In addition, there are four other full time staff and a number of part-time and casual staff are used subject to demand.

To date all the budgets had been held centrally and broken down into the following broad headings:

Expenditure
Salaries and Employee related costs
Sessional Fees
Property Costs (including utilities)
Supplies and Services
Capital Expenditure (Furniture and Equipment)
Other General Expenditure

Income
Fees and Charges for activities
Subsidies/Grants from central and local government
Fund-raising events

It is clear that each area of service requires separate budgets broken down in a way that is practical and relevant. Work has yet to be done in this area.

Given the above scenario undertake the following:

a) Identify the level to which budgets should ideally be devolved

b) Consider the possible problems that may occur with the ideal level of devolvement and give a practical solution.

Suggested solutions to this exercise can be found on page 129

Exercise 2

Devolving Budgets in your Own Organisation

If relevant, consider the following questions and make notes for your own reference.

1. At present do you have a devolved budget and what does devolvement mean in your organisation?

2. Do you consider that more or fewer budgets should be devolved, and to what levels?

3. What positive changes do you consider could be made to make devolvement more effective in your area of activity (always consider if the suggestions made are practical given the current environment)?

Chapter 3

Setting the Budget

What is a Budget?

A budget can be defined in a number of different ways. Popular definitions talk about an amount of money that can be spent on a particular item, or a projection of next year's income and expenditure. The definition that will be used in this text is "**a financial plan**". This definition is important because it emphasises the need to link finance to planned activity; the financial plan has to be part of an overall plan.

The ideal way to prepare a budget is to initially begin with the organisation's objectives by asking, "what is the organisation trying to achieve?" This principle is relevant for organisations in all sectors. A clear direction is a key factor to successful budget setting. Understanding exactly what the organisation is trying to achieve, allows the various departments and sections to establish their own objectives which are consistent with the overarching organisational goals.

Business Plans

Many organisations produce business or service plans on a regular basis. These set out organisational objectives and how they are to be achieved. A business plan should always be supported by a financial plan which sets out how finance will be generated and utilised over the period of the plan. The business plan is becoming an increasingly important tool as public sector organisations take a more "business like" approach to service delivery. The process of developing a business plan is not covered in this book, but is an ideal tool to be used as part of the budget setting process.

Budget Setting Cycle

Most publicly funded organisations are expected to prepare an annual budget to justify their funding. In many cases the approved budget is then made public to ensure transparency. It is usual for the annual budget to be prepared by a particular time each year. This may be to meet the requirements of Committees, Boards, Trustees, Funders, Grant Givers, Government, etc. In order to achieve this, many organisations establish a regular cycle of activities as part of the process of creating the budget. This is often referred to as a "budget setting cycle" which may be formally published. This should then be distributed to all those contributing to the process, to follow each year. It is important for mangers responsible for any part of the budgeting process to be familiar with the budget setting cycle. The cycle can be driven by either a top down or bottom up approach, or a mixture of the two. Both of these approaches are explained as follows:

Top Down Approach

The top down approach to the cycle is where the organisation's main decision making body establishes the broad budget parameters, e.g.

councillors in a local authority, school governors in a school, the trust board in a NHS trust, the management committee in a voluntary organisation. These parameters will include:

* *expenditure targets which may involve savings and cuts*

* *income strategies such as the level of charges, tax rates, grants*

* *use of reserves, whether to build or utilise them*

* *key priorities for services*

Having made these decisions, departments are then set cash limited budgets within which to develop their budget proposals.

Bottom Up Approach

The bottom up approach starts with the service areas or divisions setting out their plans for the year and the amount of resources needed to achieve those plans. Within public and voluntary services this is usually a "net expenditure" position which will have to be funded with some type of budget allocation. (*i.e., many public sector services do not generate any income, and those that do may not generate sufficient to cover the service costs).* This information is fed up the decision making ladder and consolidated at departmental level. At this stage, decisions on priorities have to be made to ensure the departmental budget is realistic. Changes to budgets are referred back to those who originally set the budget to make the necessary adjustments - quite often savings.

This process is continued until the department achieves a budget that reflects the divisional plans and agreement is reached over the level of financial resources required to deliver front line services. The departments will then consolidate their budgets to produce an overall organisational budget. The funding of the budget then needs to be identified and decisions made as to whether or not to raise income by charge increases, borrowing, tax increases, use of reserves, higher demands for grant income and so on. In the bottom up approach these decisions are driven by the service needs as identified at the bottom of the organisation and not the priorities set at the top.

Important aspects of the budget setting cycle include:

- *The business plan, or at least organisational objectives*
- *Fixed and variable assumptions on inflation rates, pay rates, contract terms, etc.*
- *Detailed service action plans produced, (ideally costed)*
- *Check and challenge process, where plans are scrutinised, prioritised, and if necessary changed*
- *Overall budget requirement calculated*
- *Budget availability confirmed, often subject to income targets be they from grants, taxes, rents, etc.*
- *Budget agreed and allocations given*
- *Budget sometimes formally published*
- *Timescales set for all of the above and communicated to relevant staff*

The length of the cycle tends to vary depending on the size, structure, and the levels of decision making that exist within the organisation. For example, the budget setting cycle of some local authorities stretches across the whole year, whereas in a small voluntary organisation the cycle may be complete within a few weeks.

Key Elements of a Budget

Most public sector services will have a number of budget headings relating to categories of income and expenditure. The headings will be referred to using a variety of terms such as budget heads, cost codes, etc. Even though there may be a range of expenditure and income headings, they are usually grouped together into core areas. These core areas include:

Employee Costs ⇨ Including salaries, on-costs (such as national insurance and pensions), overtime, agency fees, etc.

Accommodation costs ⇨ Including rents, rates, repairs, heat, light, etc.

Transportation Costs ⇨ Including travelling expenses, vehicle maintenance, etc.

Supplies and Services ⇨ Includes all direct revenue expenditure budgets required to operate the service, such as materials, professional fees,

		contractors fees, postage, stationery and so on.
Support Service Costs	⇨	Includes service department costs such as finance, legal, personnel, IT, etc.
Income	⇨	Charges, fees, grants, etc.

Budget Setting Techniques

There are a number of budget setting techniques that can be applied to both expenditure and income budgets. They can be used independently, or combined depending on the type of budget being set. The key techniques to be discussed are as follows:

- ***Incremental Budgeting***
- ***Zero Based Budgeting***
- ***Cash Limited Budgeting***
- ***Resource Restricted Budgeting***
- ***Activity Based Budgeting***
- ***Contingency Budgeting***

Incremental Budgeting

This technique relies on using an historic base as a starting point for budget setting. This is often the budget or the actual figures for the previous year, or some combination of the two. The base is then used to formulate the budget for the following year by taking each budget heading and either adding or subtracting an inflation factor from the base figures and adjusting for other known factors such as savings or approved growth.

An example of the incremental approach is shown as follows:

It is September and a nursery school is to develop a budget for next year. Its financial year runs from 1 April to 31 March. They have agreed the pay award at 4% for the following year with effect from 1 July of that year, and inflation is to be 3% for all other non-pay items.

Budget Heading	**Previous Year Budget Figures**	**Incremental Adjustments**	**Budget for next year**
	£	£	£
Salaries	200,000	*6,000	206,000
Food	40,000	1,200	41,200
Supplies and Services	40,000	1,200	41,200
TOTAL	**280,000**	**8,400**	**288,400**

Note: *Pay award for only 9 months of year, as only effective from 1 July.

The advantages and dis-advantages of this type of budgeting technique can be summarised as follows:

Advantages

- Simple
- Quick
- Accurate, if little change in activity

Dis-Advantages

- Historic
- No account taken of necessary future changes
- Assumes the base is accurate
- Compounds historic errors

Incremental budgeting is best used for certain items of expenditure which are unlikely to change from year to year. For example, when staffing remains constant, salaries can be budgeted for incrementally where the increment reflects the pay award, or in the case of fixed price contracts there may be an agreed annual inflation rate.

Zero Based Budgeting

This approach to budget setting is most strongly recommended as it is linked to the business planning process. The zero based budget assumes that all budgets are derived from first principles and that the organisation can start with a blank piece of paper; a zero base. They are based on the objectives to be achieved for the period without necessarily referring to the past. The key steps to be taken when using this technique are summarised as follows:

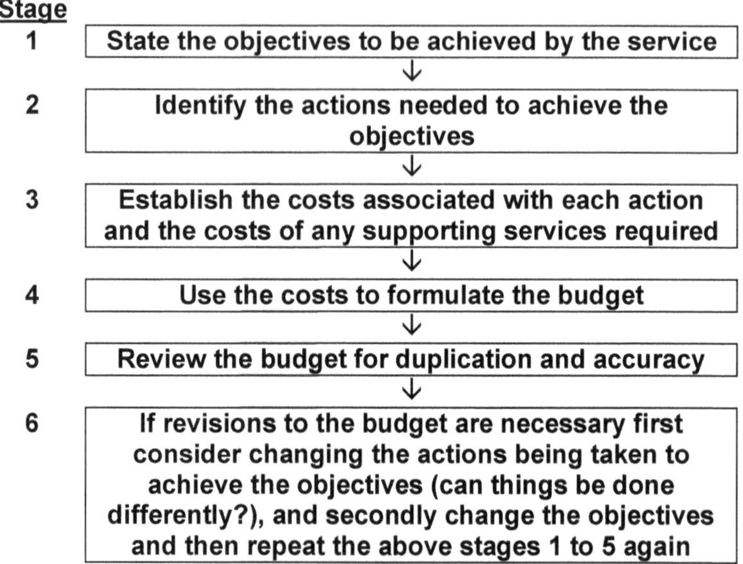

An example of the zero based approach is given below:

> It is September and a nursery school is to develop a budget for next year. Its financial year runs from 1 April to 31 March. The agreed objective for next year is to increase the level of available nursery places from 24 to 30, and to extend the range of activities offered.

Following the stages identified in diagram 2, actions needed to achieve the objective include having to increase staff by one additional nursery nurse; provide for 8 hours of agency staff per week; and to purchase more play and educational equipment to add new activities to the existing programme.
The costs of the actions are:

- *to increase salaries to reflect the additional post; agency fees; in addition to increments, pay awards and on-costs for all staff*

- *to provide for additional equipment purchases based on estimates gained from equipment suppliers*

Using the information gained above a budget can then be formulated:

Budget Heading	Budget Figures	Zero Base Assumptions
Salaries	£225,800	Salaries for 10 staff plus on costs for next year, £206,000 plus a nursery nurse @ £15,000 and agency fees based on 8 hrs. per week @ £12 per hour (assume a 50 week year).
Food	£37,500	Cost of providing breakfast, lunch and tea for 30 children @ £5 per head per day, 5 days per week, for 50 weeks.
Supplies and Services	£48,000	Estimates and contracts agreed for next year's supplies and services plus equipment purchases of £6,000.
TOTAL	**£311,300**	

The advantages and dis-advantages of this type of budgeting technique can be summarised as follows:

Advantages

- Pro-active and forward looking
- Realistic and accurate
- Links into business plans

Dis-Advantages

- Time consuming
- Requires clear objectives
- Many organisations cannot begin with a zero base as they have committed expenditure on existing staff, buildings and contracts, which they are obliged to continue, at least in the short term.

It is generally considered the advantages of zero based budgeting outweigh the dis-advantages. Where possible, zero based principles should be adopted, even when in most instances an organisation will not have a totally zero base to begin with.

Cash Limited Budgeting

This technique is appropriate when the service area is given a set limit on its total net expenditure. The service manager then has to determine what can be delivered within this cash limit, and create a budget accordingly. This technique can prove difficult if the service objectives give targets on output without reference to the practicality of meeting those targets within a cash limit. The approach to be used in the case of cash limited budgets is to identify the costs that are fixed, i.e. those that cannot be reduced, and then to spread the balance of the budget across those items which are variable and have an element of flexibility. An example of the cash limited approach is as follows:

It is September and a nursery school is to develop a budget for next year. Its financial year runs from 1 April to 31 March. They have been given a cash limited budget of £270,000 to maintain the current level of service.

Budget Heading	**Budget Figures**	**Cash Limit Calculations**
Salaries	£206,000	Salaries for 10 staff plus on costs for next year £206,000. This is a fixed cost and reflects actual salaries to be paid.
Food	£24,000	Cost of providing breakfast, lunch and tea for 24 children @ £4 per head per day for 50 weeks. Expenditure reduced to the lowest possible amount for a balanced menu.
Supplies and Services	£40,000	Fixed contract payments included and other expenditure reduced to fit the cash limit.
TOTAL	**£270,000**	

The advantages and dis-advantages of this type of budgeting technique can be summarised as follows:

Advantages
- Clear parameters on expenditure
- Quick - negotiation limited
- Incentive to make savings to bring expenditure in line with cash limit

Dis-Advantages
- Services may have to decrease quality or quantity (or both) in order to stay within the cash limit
- Not necessarily linked to business objectives which may include a need for change or development
- Assumes there is sufficient flexibility in the budget to operate within an overall cash limit
- Inflexible - not practical for demand led/statutory services

Resource Restricted Budgeting

This type of budgeting occurs when resources to be utilised by the service are restricted. Resource restriction will typically relate to:

- *Staff*
- *Equipment*
- *Property*
- *Finance (the cash limited budget is a form of resource restricted budget)*

There are often many reasons why resources need to be restricted. For example, it may be necessary for the benefit of the whole organisation to restrict staff numbers. This action may be required because recruiting an additional full time member of staff represents an on-going future commitment which the organisation may not be able to sustain. Hence, restricting the staffing resource is a common budget setting approach.

An example of the resource restricted approach is given below:

> It is September and a nursery school is to develop a budget for next year. Its financial year runs from 1 April to 31 March. Management identified the following resource restrictions. Staffing establishment should not exceed 9 full time members of staff, and supplies and services expenditure should not exceed £40,000. The current level of service should be maintained.

Budget Heading	**Budget Figures**	**Resource Restricted Calculations**
Salaries	£206,400	Salaries for 9 staff plus on costs for next year £185,400, plus agency fees to cover 35 hours per week @ £12 per hour for a 50 week year.
Food	£30,000	Cost of providing breakfast, lunch and tea for 24 children @ £5 per head per day, 5 days per week, for 50 weeks.
Supplies and Services	£40,000	Cash limited.
TOTAL	**£276,400**	

The advantages and dis-advantages of this type of budgeting technique can be summarised as follows:

Advantages

- Clear parameters on expenditure
- Quick - negotiation limited
- Organisation maintains strong control over its resources

Dis-Advantages

- No consideration of the practical impact of restricting resources and the effect on services
- Not linked to business objectives which may include a need for change or development
- Inflexible - not practical for demand led/statutory services

Activity Based Budgeting

The organisation using this approach sets budgets based on the cost of providing each area of activity. If the budget has to be reduced, each activity should be examined, and decisions made as to which should cease or reduce accordingly. This method of budgeting is only possible if there are clear divisions between each activity, and where resources can be separately allocated. Where resources are shared (such as staff, premises, etc.) the scope for activity based budgeting is more difficult. It then relies on accurate resource allocation methods, such as time charging by staff, allocating square footage, and utility usage, etc. to individual activities.

An example of activity based budgeting is given as follows:

> A nursery is about to produce an activity based budget for next year. It has identified three key areas of service:

~ Baby room services for children less than 2 years old

~ Standard nursery services for children between 2 and 3 years old

~ A nursery school service for 4 year olds

Each activity is run by different staff and based in different parts of the nursery school building. An individual budget for each activity has been used to develop the total budget for the nursery as follows:

Budget Heading	Budget Figures	Activity Based Calculations
Baby room	£85,000	Based on staff and resources utilised to provide a service for 4 children with a high staff to child ratio and lots of equipment. Apportionment is made for all shared resources such as accommodation.
Nursery	£157,500	As above but for 14 children with a lower staff ratio.
Nursery School	£52,500	As above but for 6 children with a lower staff ratio.
TOTAL	**£295,000**	

The advantages and dis-advantages of this type of budgeting technique can be summarised as follows:

Advantages

- Resources clearly matched to service provision
- Forms a base for unit costing
- Highlights which are the most expensive activities

Dis-Advantages

- Resource allocation may not be accurate
- Can be complex to calculate as detailed work needs to be undertaken to isolate each activity and the resources consumed
- Not practical for services where a flexible approach needs to be taken and where resources need to be moved between activities in response to demand

Contingency Budgeting

This budgeting technique is sometimes seen as "a broad brush" approach. Limited effort is used to establish detailed estimates for each of the budget headings as a contingency amount is provided to take account of poor estimates, changes in demand, and insufficient resources. The contingency may be used flexibly across any of the budget headings. The level of the contingency will depend on an estimation of the risk of error within the budget. If it is considered that the budget has been calculated to an accuracy level of 80%, then a 20% contingency may be added to the budget.

An example of the contingency approach is given as follows:

It is September and a nursery school is to develop a budget for next year. It's financial year runs from 1 April to 31 March.

Budget Heading	Budget Figures	Contingency Calculations
Salaries	£200,000	Salaries for approximately 10 staff and some agency time if needed.
Food	£40,000	Approximate food expenditure last year.
Supplies and Services	£40,000	Approximate expected expenditure
Contingency	£20,000	Will be used to supplement overspent budgets.
TOTAL	**£300,000**	

The advantages and dis-advantages of this type of budgeting technique can be summarised as follows:

Advantages
- Quick
- Easy
- Flexible

Dis-Advantages
- Inaccurate; open to guess work
- Insufficient thought given to linking service with finance
- Will be difficult to monitor

Application of Budget Setting Techniques

Having considered a number of budget setting techniques, it is clear that a combination of all these techniques may be utilised in creating a budget. For example:

Salaries

Incremental budgeting may be suitable if there is no change in establishment or if there is a resource restriction which states that staffing should remain constant.

Accommodation

Rent and rates are usually fixed in nature and therefore could be subject to a cash limited or resource restricted budget.

Supplies and Services

These usually vary from year to year dependent upon what the organisation is trying to achieve. Often some of the budgets in this category are demand led and therefore difficult to predict. This will require a zero based approach with the addition of a contingency budget if the budget area is extremely volatile.

Income

Usually income will consist of fees and charges often related to specific activities. In this case an activity based approach to setting the budget may be the most appropriate.

Profiling Budgets

In addition to setting an annual budget it is also important to "profile" the budget. Profiling involves estimating how income and expenditure will arise over the year; for example, taking into account seasonal variations. The budget profile is fundamental to effective budget monitoring which will be discussed in the next chapter. For example, a budget profile for salaries should reflect the increments, pay awards and the known leavers and joiners during the year. A salary profile can be shown graphically as follows:

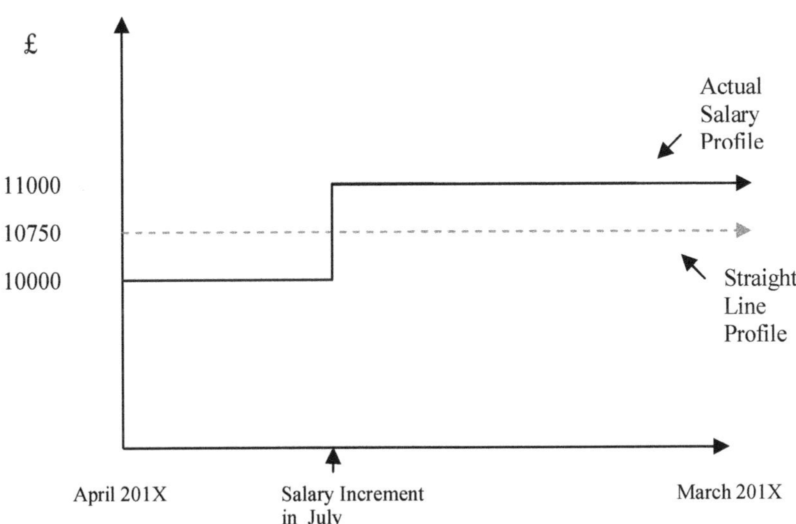

The previous graph shows that salaries increase from £10,000 per month to £11,000 per month as from July 201X onwards, giving a total salary budget of £129,000. This is represented in the diagram by the solid line.

However, some organisations regularly profile expenditure budgets equally across the twelve months of the year; this is referred to as a "straight line" profile. The dashed line in the diagram represents a straight line profile for the same £129,000 salary budget, resulting in a monthly budget of £10,750. If the straight line approach is taken, it is quite evident that every month the actual spend will differ from the straight line budget profile, thus creating a monthly variance. Where possible these types of profiling differences should be eliminated and therefore improve the budget monitoring process.

Common Budget Setting Practices

There are a number of budget setting practices which are commonly adopted by many public sector organisations. Some of these practices are highlighted below.

Vacancy factor/discount

It is quite common to calculate the total salary budget and then to reduce the budget by a vacancy factor. The logic behind this budgeting technique is that during the year there will always be a turnover of staff, and hence there will always be a percentage of vacant posts. However, depending on the economic climate, employees may stay in their posts for far longer, therefore reducing the level of staff turnover. In these circumstances the scope for making savings through a vacancy factor is clearly more restricted.

Mid-point Salary Scales

In an organisation that uses scale rate salaries for graded posts, a common budgeting technique for salaries is to adopt the mid-point of the salary scale. The logic is that this represents a good approximation of the average for all staff and therefore is an acceptable way of calculating a salary estimate. However, if most staff are at the top of their salary scale, this technique can result in a large under estimate of the salary budget.

Base Budgets

A base budget is sometimes called an "original budget". Each year changes from the base budget are made usually using an incremental technique and adjustments made for any major changes. In the following year, the adjustments are usually eliminated in order to return to the original base budget. This is an historic approach to budget setting and in some instances the assumptions behind the base budget may have been lost or forgotten and can be very far re-moved from the reality of current service requirements.

Guess Work

Budgets for many items are often estimated using an educated guess. Ideally budgets should be based on written quotations, contract values, payroll information, etc. There should be very few areas that need to rely solely on guess work.

Arbitrary apportionment

Most budget estimates will have an element of this insofar as there will be central costs that need to be shared across different services. Even though there will be a need for apportionment, it should, where possible, be based on service use and not arbitrary methods. Apportionment methods include number of employees, floor area, budget size, and so on.

Summary

- A budget is a financial plan
- Budgets should ideally be linked to the business plan and be based on the organisation's objectives for the coming year
- Many organisations have a budget setting cycle identifying when the stages of the budget setting process takes place
- Budget setting may be top down; bottom up; or a combination of the two depending on the level of devolvement within an organisation
- A number of budgeting techniques can be used when setting a budget. These include, incremental; zero based; cash limited; resource restricted; activity based; and contingency budgeting. It is quite possible to use elements of all these techniques when preparing a budget
- Budgets need to be profiled in order to assist with effective budgetary control
- Guess work should be kept to a minimum!

Exercise 3

Developing a Budget from First Principles

Take one of the following areas:

~A leisure centre
~A secondary school
~A meals on wheels service
~A residential nursing home
~A contracts management unit
~An advice centre
~A personnel department
~A quality assurance division
~A hospital
~A fire brigade

a) For the area selected what are the first steps that you would take to prepare a zero based budget?

List Action Points Below:

b) In order to construct the budget, what would be the key income/expenditure items for the activity and how would you obtain the information in order to budget for them accurately?

List Key Income/Expenditure Areas	What Information would you need and where from?

c) Taking the complete list of services shown on the previous page, rank the activities in terms of their ease of budget setting in the order of 1 to 10, where 1 is the easiest.

Suggested solutions to this exercise can be found on page 132

Exercise 4

Incremental Budgeting

You are a budget manager and are responsible for input to the budget preparation.

You are required to produce some budget working papers as part of the preparation for the coming year's budget. The assumptions you have made in order to prepare the budget working papers are set out as follows.

ASSUMPTIONS FOR BUDGET PREPARATION

Your team consists of the following staff members:

Yourself, J Brown	(Basic Salary £40,000)
A Taylor	(Basic Salary £30,000)
P Pritkash	(Basic Salary £22,000)
C Doyle	(Basic Salary £20,000)
O Obayo	(Basic Salary £18,000)
D Lincoln	(Basic Salary £15,000)
R Cohen	(Basic Salary £13,200)

The negotiated pay awards for next year have been agreed as a percentage of basic salary with effect from 1 July. The percentages are as follows:

Salary Band	£35,000 and above	2.0%
Salary Band	£20,000 to £35,000	2.5%

Salary Band	Under £20,000	1.5%

National Insurance is calculated at 10.45%
Pension contributions are 6%

Other budgets will be based on last year's figures which are summarised as follows:

Transport costs	£10,000
Premises costs	£50,000
Supplies and Services	£80,000
Financing costs	£10,000

The inflation rate used for the transport, premises and supplies and services budget is 3%. Finance costs are to be inflated by 1%.

Assume the financial year runs from 1 April to 31 March

There is a new development you wish to implement this year to enhance the level of customer care. The development will require an on-line computer system and training for staff in telephone skills. The total cost should be calculated as follows:

- Five upgrades to existing terminals @ £1000 each
- A systems support hotline @ £2000 for the year additional administration of service £3000 per year

- Systems training for 5 staff @ £500 each

- Telephone skills training for 5 staff @ £200 each

A pro-forma budget working paper is set out on the following page for calculation purposes.

Suggested solutions to this exercise can be found on page 134

BUDGET WORKING PAPERS

Employee Costs

Name	Basic Pay	Pay Award	Total	Nat. Ins.	Pension	Budget
TOTAL						

Operational Costs

	Costs Last Year		Inflation		Budget
Transport Costs					
Premises Costs					
Supplies and Services					
New Developments					
Financing Costs					
TOTAL					
TOTAL BUDGET					

Exercise 5

Profiling Budgets

Using the spreadsheet at the end of this exercise, profile the following budget heads and set out the projected monthly income and expenditure position (assume the financial year is 1 April to 31 March).

Salaries:
Based on current total staffing costs of £480,000 (inclusive), a pay award of 2% is due with effect from 1 July. One member of staff currently earning £36,000 (inclusive) is due to retire at the end of August and will not be replaced.

Central Recharges:
These will be based on Service Level Agreements for central services and will be charged quarterly. The total amount for the year has been estimated at £80,000.

Supplies and Services:
The total budget for these services is £60,000, however, there is no historic information on how expenditure arises for these items.

Transport Costs:
It is usual that only 25% of the total budget is spent in the first half of the year and 75% in the second

half of the year. The total budget for transport is £18,000.

Professional Fees:

These arise on an adhoc basis as and when they are needed. It is difficult to predict the level of expenditure each year as it fluctuates tremendously based on the case loads. A total budget of £120,000 has been set, with a view that the contingency budget may have to be used.

Contingency:

A contingency has been established as part of the budget this year. This is in order to provide for incorrect estimates, unforeseen events, and fluctuating demand. The total contingency allowed for the year has been set at 10% of all expenditure heads.

Fees:

Having examined historic records and spoken to internal customers, an estimate for fees has been established at approximately £900,000. It has been assumed that fees will arise equally over the year as a basis for profiling.

Suggested solutions to this exercise can be found on page 135

PROFILED BUDGET

	Apr	May	Jun	Jul	Aug	Sep	Oct	Nov	Dec	Jan	Feb	Mar	Total
INCOME													
Fees													
Total													
EXPENDITURE													
Salaries													
Central Recharges													
Supplies and Services													
Transport Costs													
Professional Fees													
Contingency													
TOTAL													
Surplus/Deficit Month													

Exercise 6

Budget Setting in your Organisation

a) Describe the current budget setting process and your involvement with the process.

b) Who is responsible for agreeing the final budget and when are you made aware of your budget?

c) How could the budget setting process be improved? This includes from initial stages through to the issue of the final budget.

Chapter 4

Budgetary Control

Budgetary control is about managing the monies allocated to a particular budget, as well as ensuring that funds are properly utilised with respect to the level, and quality, of output required from those resources.

For example:

> *If questioned, many budget holders would say they are capable of managing a furniture budget of £10,000, meaning they would ensure the budget was not over spent. However, this is only one aspect of budget management. In order to fully manage the budget, the budget holder needs to know what the £10,000 budget was expected to purchase (quantity and quality) and over what time frame.*
>
> *If the objectives for the £10,000 furniture budget are to purchase 100 specialist chairs without arms, of average quality over the next three months, the budget holder may then begin to manage the budget. The budget holder will not just monitor the amount of money being spent on the chairs during the period, but also the number of chairs being purchased, and the quality of those chairs.*

The budget holder may consider they have performed well if the correct number and quality of chairs have been purchased for less than £10,000.

Therefore, in order to adequately manage a budget, the budget holder has to know both the quantity of service/product to be provided and the quality standard that needs to be met. Budgetary control will then involve monitoring the money, the quantity and quality of the output.

Monitoring and Managing the Budget

To ensure effective budgetary control, budgets have to be monitored and managed. In some organisations these functions are separated. If the budgets are delegated, then the budget holder may only undertake monitoring with no real power to manage the budget. If the budget is fully devolved, then the budget holder will both monitor and manage the budget. The difference between monitoring and managing budgets is not clearly defined, however, they can be broadly distinguished as follows:

Monitoring Budgets ⇨ Checking accuracy of actual income and expenditure; comparing actuals with budgets; comparing actual with expected outputs; identifying trends; highlighting areas of over and under spending to the person managing the budget.

Managing Budgets ⇨ As a result of detailed monitoring, taking the necessary action to ensure the budget remains in control.

Just how much ability a budget holder has to both monitor and manage will depend on the decision making structure within the organisation.

Budgetary Control Process

The process of controlling budgets can be broken down into a number of stages:

Establish Actual Position

There will be a need to examine the financial management information available within the organisation. (The range of relevant financial information is discussed in chapter 5). Depending on the quality of reports produced, there may be a need for other records to be maintained, sometimes by the budget holder or front-line staff. The actual position will have to take account of "committed" expenditure. (See commitment accounting later in this chapter).

Compare Actual with Budget

The difference between the actual and budgeted figures results in a "variance". Variance analysis is an important tool in the budgetary control process. Variance analysis is discussed in detail in the next section.

Establish Reasons for Variances

There are a number of reasons why the actual and budgeted figures differ. The reasons for any variance need to be identified. This process is critical to gaining effective control as the budget holder needs to know when it is appropriate to take corrective action.

Take Action

Budgets are only being managed if action is taken to control them. There are a number of actions that a budget holder may take to establish effective control. These are set out later in this chapter.

Variance Analysis

In the context of budgetary control, the term variance refers to the difference between actual and budget. An example of a variance is shown as follows:

Month 6			
Budget Heading	**Budget to Date**	**Actual to Date**	**Variance**
Salaries	£120,000	£132,000	(£12,000)

The above example shows that by the six month period, the budgeted expenditure on salaries was £120,000, however, actual spending on salaries for those six months totalled £132,000. The difference between these two figures is £12,000 which represents the variance from the budget. In this case the variance is negative, hence the brackets, representing an overspend.

Budget to date will show the amount of the budget that should have been spent by month 6. Ideally the budget will be profiled to reflect the pattern of spending over the year such that when actual expenditure for the period is compared with the budget, the true variance is calculated.

A more comprehensive variance statement is shown below.

Month 6								
Budget	**Budget for the month**	**Actual for the month**	**Variance**	**%**	**Budget to Date**	**Actual to Date**	**Variance**	**%**
Salaries	50,000	53,000	(3,000)	6	120,000	132,000	(12,000)	10

This statement shows the variance for the month as well as the year to date. The variance for the month is often referred to as the **discrete** as opposed to the year to date which is referred to as the **cumulative**.

Variances can be expressed in terms of figures or percentages. A budget holder needs to know the amount of over or under spend, however, it is also useful to know what proportion of the budget has been over or under-spent. The over or under spend could be a large amount but only represent a small proportion of the total budget. The action taken as a result of a variance will depend on both its amount and proportion in relation to the budget.

Establishing Actuals

In order to establish a true variance, it is important that the actual expenditure recorded is accurate. Actual expenditure at any particular point in time will include the following elements:

- *Goods and services that have been paid for*
- *Goods and services that have been used but not paid for. These items may be represented by invoices unpaid (creditors), or by accruals (estimates of amounts used during the period even though invoices have not yet been received, e.g. telephone bills)*

All actual expenditure should be charged to the budget heading to which it relates. If the budget has been correctly constructed, there should be little difficulty in identifying where the actual expenditure should be charged.

It is usual for an accounting system to be used whereby codes are allocated to each budget heading. Many organisations operate computerised accounting systems which allocate the actual expenditure to the code or codes given. Ideally, the budget holder should be responsible for the coding, even if it is undertaken by someone else. At the very minimum, the budget holder should be aware of the codes that have been allocated to each of the budget headings under their control and should ensure that actual expenditure is always correctly coded.

Commitment Accounting

In order to have a full awareness of their true position, a budget holder should know not only the actual expenditure at any point in time, but also what expenditure has been committed at that point. Committed expenditure relates to elements of the budget that have been formerly allocated to future expenditure such as "orders" or "contracts". By calculating the committed expenditure, the budget holder is able to identify the true "remaining balance" of a budget. This will also impact on the variance calculation against planned expenditure. Commitment accounting will provide the budget holder with a tighter control of the budget and will throw greater light on the reasons for variances as commitments tend to reflect future activities.

In order to operate a commitment accounting system, it is important to have a method of identifying goods and services that have been committed to. This is usually achieved by way of an order, contract, etc. which commits the organisation to purchase goods or use services.

Reasons for Variances

There are a number of reasons why variances occur, the most common of which are identified as follows:

Mis-coding	»	Wrong account code used
Error	»	Incorrect figures entered onto the accounting system
Delays	»	Delays in entering information onto the accounting system
Profiling	»	Often incorrect budget profiles are entered which bear no relevance to the pattern of actual expenditure (e.g. no

		account taken of seasonal fluctuations)
Poor budgeting	»	Little consideration given to initial budget preparation
Unplanned changes	»	Such as increases and decreases in demand for services, or introduction of new legislation
Poor management	»	Where a budget has been properly prepared but badly managed. For example, lights are left on 24 hours a day causing waste and hence overspending of the electric budget. Conversely, good management may lead to budget savings

Projecting the Outturn

In order to fully control the budget, it is necessary to remain focussed on the future position. The calculation of the **outturn** becomes an important process as it reflects the projected financial position at the end of the year. The projected outturn should be calculated on a regular basis taking into account assumptions about changes to the budgeted expenditure during the year.

An illustration of how the projected outturn may be calculated is shown as follows:

Financial Management Report – Month 6					
Account Description	**Total Budget**	**Budget to Date**	**Actual to Date**	**Projected Outturn**	**Project (over)/ underspend for year**
Salaries	250,000	125,000	135,000	270,000	(20,000)

The projected outturn of £270,000 in the above example assumes that spending continues into the second six months at the same rate as in the previous six months. This projection is based on an even arithmetic progression over the 12 months and a general formula for this type of calculation is given as follows:

$$\frac{\text{Amount Spent to Date}}{\text{Number of months to Date}} \quad \text{X} \quad 12 \quad = \quad \text{Projected Outturn}$$

If a budget has extremely variable expenditure each month, or where there are known future changes with respect to the budget, both these aspects need to be taken into account when calculating the projected outturn. Using the above example, if it is known that a member of staff is leaving the organisation, the projected outturn should be adjusted downwards to reflect the salary reduction. If there are no adjustments, the projected outturn should continue to reflect the original expenditure profile of the budget.

Virement

This is a common word used in the public sector and refers to a particular process which can be used in the following ways:

- *the establishment of new budgets*

- *the amendment of an existing budget*

The process involves moving funds from one budget heading to another budget heading and so is only possible if there is a budget to vire from. For example, if there is a clothing budget of £3,000 and no budget for equipment, it would be possible to vire an amount from the clothing budget, say £1,500, and establish an equipment budget. Virements are used for corrective action whereby a budget that has been under spent can be used to increase a budget that has been overspent. The effect of this is to change the budgeted amounts for each area to more accurately reflect the current spending position.

Taking Corrective Action

There are a number of actions that can be taken by a budget holder when attempting to control an over or under spent budget. These include:

For Budget Overspend	For Budget Under spend
▪ Reduce or halt expenditure ▪ Increase income ▪ Make virements ▪ Use contingency funds ▪ Delay activities ▪ Re-define objective ▪ Re-define eligibility criteria ▪ Change nature of the service ▪ Cease or reduce service delivery	▪ Increase expenditure (particularly on efficiency improvements) ▪ Make virements ▪ Save or increase contingency funds ▪ Bring forward activities ▪ Re-define objectives ▪ Re-define eligibility criteria ▪ Change the nature of the service (e.g. quality improvements) ▪ Increase service delivery

Whilst a great deal of emphasis is usually given to the prevention of overspending, underspending on budgets can be equally as bad. If as a result of the underspend objectives and service targets have not been met, there could be serious implications, such as:

- *future budget reductions*
- *lost income*
- *funders withdrawing future support*
- *other providers being brought in who can deliver on time and on budget*

Controllable and Uncontrollable Budgets

The following diagram illustrates the process for identifying an uncontrollable budget.

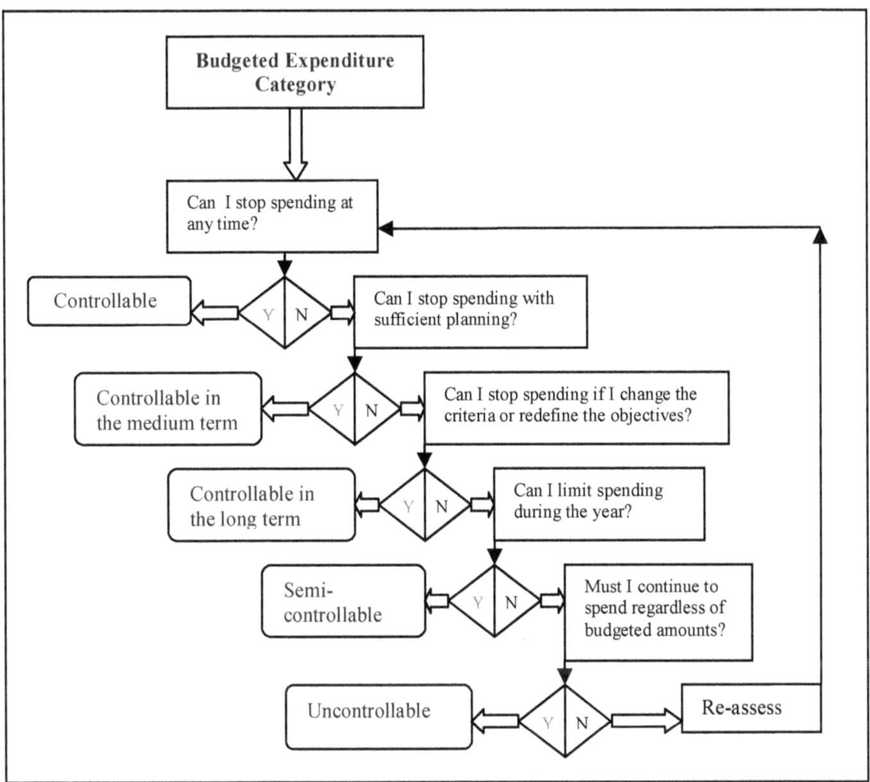

It is relatively straight forward to identify actions that may be taken with respect to controllable budgets; many of the actions on the previous page are relevant. However, in the case of uncontrollable budgets, where there is an overspend, the action may be to identify compensating savings from controllable budgets. This scenario can arise when there is a demand led statutory service which cannot be halted in the short term, regardless of the level of spending. Funding of the overspend will often be at the expense of reductions in expenditure on non-statutory controllable activities.

Controlling Income Budgets

Income budgets should be based on a detailed income forecast which clearly identifies where each source of income is to be found. Income budgets which rely heavily on user contributions, such as leisure centre entrance fees, are generally more difficult to control. In such cases the income budget is fundamental to overall budgetary control and requires considerable management. It should be remembered, an underperformance on income is equivalent to overspending on an expenditure budget. In order to adequately control income, the following issues are important:

- *Ensure that a detailed monthly projection has been produced that is correctly profiled based on past experience and future expectation*
- *Regular projected outturns should be calculated*
- *Where applicable, the marketing plan needs to be closely allied to expected income targets arising from marketing activities. Marketing plans need to be changed if income targets are not being met*
- *Original income estimates should always be prudently developed due to the unpredictable nature of certain types of income*

- *If income is to be a fixed amount under contract, the contract terms need to be monitored*

- *If there is a trend of under-achievement on income, the corrective action steps should be taken as previously listed*

Summary

- Budgetary control is not only about controlling the money, it is also about controlling the output resulting from the financial resource input
- Effective budgetary control involves both monitoring and managing the budget
- The budgetary control process compares actual spending with budgeted spending and takes action to correct variations
- Commitment accounting takes into account expenditure that has been committed such as orders for goods and services
- Projecting the outturn is a useful budgetary control technique which should be regularly undertaken so as to provide an up to date assessment of the year end position
- Corrective action should be taken if actual spending is very different from the budget. This would include actions such as virements
- Income budgets require as much control as expenditure budgets

Exercise 7

Variance Analysis

1. Give your interpretation of the following variances; examine each line independently.

Month 6 Report (September)

		Actual	Budget	Variance	Actual YTD	Budget YTD	Variance YTD
a)	Salaries	2200	2000	-200	12200	12000	-200
b)	Salaries	2000	2000	0	12000	12000	0
c)	Salaries	2200	2000	-200	13200	12000	-1200
d)	Salaries	1200	2000	800	12200	12000	-200
e)	Salaries	2400	2000	-400	12200	12000	-200
f)	Salaries	2000	2000	0	12400	12000	-400
g)	Salaries	1800	2000	200	11800	12000	200

2. Give four examples of what may cause a variance in your area of work.
3. Give two examples of uncontrollable variances in your area of work.
4. As a budget holder, what key control mechanisms could you apply to bring variances under control.

Suggested solutions to this exercise can be found on page 136

Exercise 8

The Role of the Budget Holder

You have been given the responsibility for a furniture budget for the entire office which includes four separate floors with each floor housing a separate division. The budget has been cash limited at £40,000 for the year. This figure has been developed by the accountant who took last year's budget and applied zero growth. As budget holder you are responsible for approving all expenditure on furniture and requests have to be made to you by the divisional heads.

In the past there has been wide disgruntlement for several reasons

- *There appeared to be no control of the budget as it was always spent by month 6, and anyone who had not ordered furniture in the first half of the year had to go without*

- *Some divisions had substantially more spent on them than others regardless of their relative size*

- *There appeared to be no choice in the type of furniture received, e.g. chairs always came in the same colour regardless of the one ordered due to "bulk" purchasing*

- *The budget was not previously devolved to a particular person and was administered by finance on a first come first served basis with no assessment of need*

- *Some divisions think suppliers were paid for furniture that was never actually received. Deliveries are usually made directly to the division in question, and invoices are sent separately to the finance department for payment, who never appeared to check goods were received*

As the new budget holder you are determined to ensure that such complaints cease and that the budget is properly managed. There have been rumours that performance related pay increments will be linked to how well budgets are managed and so you have a personal interest in the whole process.

Questions:

a) What steps do you think need to be taken from the beginning of the year to ensure the budget is well controlled?

b) What systems need to be in place to assist the budget holder to maintain control during the year?

c) How will the budget holder manage to stop the complaints this year?

Suggested solutions to this exercise can be found on page 139

Exercise 9

Budgetary Control in Your Organisation

1) Describe the current process of budgetary control in your organisation?

2) How are you involved in the control process?

3) Do you consider budgets are adequately controlled in all areas within your organisation, and if not, how do you consider budgetary control can be improved?

Chapter 5

Financial Management Information

A financial management information system (FMIS) is used to record and process transactions of a financial nature, and then to provide financial information.

Financial information arising from FMIS's is used for a variety of purposes. Most typically it is used as the basis for preparing the annual "audited financial accounts", as well as providing on-going management accounting information.

The financial accounts are sometimes required by legislation, funders, or demanded as a condition of financial support. They are audited by an independent agency or firm of accountants who report on the fairness of the financial information produced. The audited accounts are available to the public and can often be found on an organisation's website.

In contrast, the management accounts are produced for internal users only, and provide information for the day to day management and control of an organisation's finances.

The key difference between the audited financial accounts and the internally focused management accounts are highlighted as follows:

FINANCIAL ACCOUNTS	MANAGEMENT ACCOUNTS
❖ *Standard financial statements which have to be prepared in a recognised format*	❖ *Tailor made statements and reports which can be presented in any format as desired by the user*
❖ *External orientation, as they will be available in the public domain*	❖ *Internal orientation, as they should only be seen by the user of the information*
❖ *Required by law to be prepared on a regular basis - annually*	❖ *Prepared as often as deemed useful – could be daily reports*
❖ *Reports on the past. Accounts are prepared on a historic basis reporting transactions and activities that have already taken place*	❖ *Looks to the future. Management accounts contain budgetary information for the year ahead and considers how past activities will impact on budgets in the future*
❖ *Tends to cover a broad area of activity*	❖ *Tends to cover a specific area of activity*
❖ *Reports have to conform to external standards*	❖ *Reports only conform to internal standards within the organisation, if they exist*

Of the above, a budget holder will typically require the management accounting information on an on-going basis to control their budget.

Management Accounts

Ideally, the management accounts that are produced by the FMIS should display the following characteristics (AEIOU).

Accurate
Easy to understand
Informative
On time
Up-to-date

Each of these attributes are discussed further on the following pages:

Accurate

It is important that financial management information is accurate and can be relied upon otherwise its integrity will fall into disrepute, and the information may be disregarded by the users. Accuracy is achieved by ensuring the information entering the FMIS is correctly processed. For example, the payment of an invoice will only be accurately entered onto the system if:

- the arithmetic is checked
- the description of the goods or service has been checked as correct and received
- the allocation of the payment is correct and goes against the appropriate budget
- the payment is authorised

Easy to understand

Management accounts are often prepared for budget holders who have little or no formal financial training. Management accounts therefore need to be set out in a simple format that can be easily understood.

Informative

In addition to being very clear, the information contained in the accounts should be relevant to budget holders and provide the information necessary to control their budgets. The type and format of information contained in the management accounts will vary depending on the type of service being managed and the budget holders own preferences. For example, some budget holders prefer variances to be stated as percentages as opposed to being shown as a positive or negative figure. Variances are discussed in detail in chapter 4.

On time

Budget holders require regular information in order to exercise adequate control. It is normal for management accounts to be produced on a regular basis, often monthly, but management accounts may be required more frequently for some budgets. It is necessary for the providers of the information to work to a timetable such that budget holders can rely on information being available when they need it. In some organisations there is sufficient flexibility for reports to be produced on demand, otherwise it is normal for monthly reports to be produced a specified number of days after the month end.

Up to date

Budget holders need to be aware of how current their management accounting information is. For example, if the management accounting report is dated September, it would be expected, as a minimum standard, that all the financial transactions up until the end of August were reflected on the report. In some cases, an organisation's management accounting information may not be up to date due to the type of systems operated, and the speed of data processing. Ideally public sector organisations should have "real time" systems which are accessible by budget holders, providing the most up to date information at any point in time.

Reporting Styles

Management accounts may be presented in a range of styles to meet the needs of the budget holder. An example of a report for a residential home is shown as follows:

Budgetary Control Report - Month 9

Cost Centre LH635 | **Lodge House**

1	2	3	4	5	6	7	8	9	10	11
Prev. Yr Actuals	Acc. No.	Acc. Name	Budget Yr	Budget YTD	Exp./Inc YTD	Variance YTD	Variance %	O/S Commit	Total + Commit	Total Spend %
		Employee Cost								
112500	A101	Salaries	110000	82500	84000	-1500	-1.8%	0	84000	76.4%
64000	A105	Wages	50000	37500	35000	2500	6.7%	0	35000	70.0%
12500	A112	Temp. Staff	2000	1500	10000	-8500	-566.7%	1000	11000	550.0%
1500	A220	Subsistence	0	0	1000	-1000	n/a	200	1200	n/a
190500	**A500**	**Sub-Total**	**162000**	**121500**	**130000**	**-8500**	**-7.0%**	**1200**	**131200**	**81.0%**
		Premises Cost								
10000	D101	Rent & Rates	10000	7500	0	7500	100.0%	0	0	0.0%
4000	D210	Utilities	4200	3150	3500	-350	-11.1%	200	3700	88.1%
750	D312	Cleaning	600	450	750	-300	-66.7%	50	800	133.3%
250	D420	Sundry	200	150	250	-100	-66.7%	0	250	125.0%
15000	**D500**	**Sub-Total**	**15000**	**11250**	**4500**	**6750**	**60.0%**	**250**	**4750**	**31.7%**
		Supplies								
4000	F210	Equipment	3000	2250	0	2250	100.0%	0	0	0.0%
1200	F305	Print & Stat.	1000	750	500	250	33.3%	0	500	50.0%
13000	F402	Provisions	12000	9000	10000	-1000	-11.1%	2000	12000	100.0%
1000	F444	Clothing	1000	750	800	-50	-6.7%	200	1000	100.0%
19200	**F500**	**Sub-Total**	**17000**	**12750**	**11300**	**1450**	**11.4%**	**2200**	**13500**	**79.4%**
224700	**Total Expenditure**		**194000**	**145500**	**145800**	**-300**	**-0.2%**	**3650**	**149450**	**77.0%**
		Income								
180000	R300	Charges	195000	146250	135000	-11250	-7.7%	0	135000	69.2%
180000	**Total Income**		**195000**	**146250**	**135000**	**-11250**	**-7.7%**	**0**	**135000**	**69.2%**
44700	**Net Expenditure/ Income (-)***		**-1000**	**-750**	**10800**	**-11550**		**3650**	**14450**	

**Net expenditure/income (-) = difference between total expenditure and total income. Hence, the budget year, shows net income of £1,000 (surplus) and year to date £750 (surplus). However, the actual expenditure to date shows a net expenditure (overspend) of £10,800 resulting in an unfavourable variance for the period of £11,550.*

The report shows a number of columns which are explained as follows:

Column No.	Column Heading
1	**Previous Year Actuals** States the actual expenditure and income figures for the previous year by cost centre.
2	**Account Number** Provides a unique code for each expenditure and income account heading. Some codes may be unique to the cost centre whilst other codes are the same for all cost centres. This allows for aggregation and consolidation of budgetary information for a number of different cost centres in order to present financial information for a whole service, or for the whole organisation.
3	**Account Name** This gives an abbreviated description of the account, and the type of expenditure which should relate to the account code.
4	**Budget for the Year** This gives the budget for the current financial year. This is one of many terms that can be used to describe this element of a report. Other terms include *annual budget; annual estimate; forecast year.*

5 **Budget Year to Date (YTD)**

This identifies how much of the budget should have been spent (or achieved in the case of income) to date. Ideally this column should be profiled according to planned expenditure and income over the twelve month period, reflecting fluctuations due to timing differences and so on. This is often referred to as the profiled budget.

6 **Expenditure/Income Year to Date (YTD)**

This shows the actual cumulative figure for the period. As the report is for month 9, this column represents 9 months of expenditure and income.

7 **Variance Year to Date (YTD)**

This shows the difference between the amount that was budgeted for the first 9 months, column 5, and the amount that was actually spent/received column 6. The variance shows whether there was an over or under performance on the budget. This can be used to highlight budgets that may be overspent at the end of the year.

8 **Variance Percentage**

This produces a calculation which takes column 7 and divides it by column 5, multiplying through by 100 to obtain the percentage. As with the variance, displaying the variance percentage highlights the extent to which the budget is under/over spent. From the report it is apparent there is a large overspend on the temporary staff budget. The percentage overspend on the subsistence budget cannot be calculated in this manner, as there was no original budget for this area of expenditure.

9 **Outstanding Commitments**

One of the purposes of this column is to identify items that have been ordered but not yet received. When the budget holder orders goods, an amount equal to the order value can be established as a commitment. The commitment is then cancelled when the invoice is received and paid. The use of this column helps the budget holder to obtain a better understanding of what is actually available to spend.

10 **Total including Commitments**

This takes the total payments to date in column 6 and adds it to the commitments in column 9. This total that is then used in column 11 to show the percentage of budget that has been spent and committed to date.

11 **Percentage Spend**

This calculates column 10 as a percentage of column 4, i.e. the total spend plus commitments, divided by the total budget. Given this is a month 9 report, it would be reasonable to expect that each heading was approximately 75% spent. However, it can be seen that some items are in excess of, or below 75%.

It should be noted that the report raises some interesting anomalies:

- **Expenditure is coded to accounts where no budget has been allocated, for example, subsistence:** *This could occur due to poor planning, e.g. when a budget head which should have been created has been forgotten, or if an error has arisen as a result of a mis-coding*

- **Budgets exist for which no actual spend has occurred, for example rents and rates:** *Again, this could be due to poor planning when budget heads which are now redundant have not been deleted, or due to mis-coding of legitimate budget spend elsewhere*

Using the Financial Management Information

Budgetary control reports should provide the budget holder with useful information that can be utilised for decision making. In particular, reports should highlight key points such as:

- *Which accounts are under or overspent*
- *How much of the budget has been spent so far*
- *Whether current expenditure is in line with planned expenditure - i.e. the budget profiles*
- *How does current expenditure compare with last year's actual expenditure*

- *The potential to make virements from one expenditure budget to another*

(The same points are relevant for income budgets)

The extent to which the reported information can be relied upon depends largely on the quality of information entered onto the FMIS. For example, budget profiles may be incorrect; items may have been incorrectly coded; or the information may be very out of date. Ideally, budget holders should have easy access to the FMIS, and in the case of a computerised system, they should have the ability to directly interrogate information.

Management accounts will be produced in a wide variety of formats depending largely on individual user requirements. However, in all cases, the budget holder will require the following basic information:

Account Information	⇨	Including account name, description, account code, and so on
Budget and Actual Information	⇨	Including total budgets, period budgets (monthly/quarterly), and profiled budgets, plus income/expenditure figures for the same periods
Variance Analysis	⇨	Showing the difference between actual and planned expenditure/income, either in total monetary terms, or as a percentage, or both

Ideally, budget holders should provide input into the report format to ensure the desired information requirements are achieved from the report. Many budget holders require the production of additional information such as statistics and details of activity in order to further assist in the interpretation of performance. Examples of additional information produced for budget holders include:

- *Percentage of budget spent to date compared with previous year*
- *Percentage of over and under spend on each budget*
- *Average spend per day or per month*
- *Average spend per client; per transaction; per employee; or any relevant activity. For example, the budget holder in a fire service, may wish to know average spend per call out, or average spend per fire, etc.*
- *Monthly spending trends showing percentage increases/decreases month on month*

If the budget holder is also responsible for achieving income targets, then similar statistics to those produced for expenditure should also be developed.

Summary

- ❑ Financial management information systems are used to record transactions of a financial nature, and to provide financial information

- ❑ Financial management information acts as a basis for the production of annual audited accounts as well as management accounts

- ❑ Financial management information should ideally have the AEIOU characteristics

- ❑ Financial reports can be presented in a variety of styles. The benefit of management accounting is that the financial information is designed to meet the needs of the budget holder

- ❑ Budget holders should ideally input into the design of the report format. In addition, budget holders may require information such as statistics and details of activity in order to fully interpret performance

Exercise 10

Understanding Financial Management Information

You have been given the management accounts of a school for children with special needs to review (shown on the following page).

a) *What is your initial reaction to the range of variances and what immediate additional information do you require in order to assist in your decision making about the variances?*

b) *Given that it is month 6 (half way through the financial year), what actions do you expect to be taken in the short term, and what actions would you expect to take in the long term?*

c) *What management techniques should be used when attempting to get the suggested actions implemented by other staff?*

d) *What other monitoring processes would you adopt in order to satisfactorily take control of the situation?*

XYZ School
Management Accounts

	Month 6 Actual	Month 6 Budget	Variance	U/F	Notes	YTD Actual	YTD Budget	Variance	U/F
INCOME									
Fees	8000	14000	-6000	U		54000	84000	-30000	U
Revenue Grant	10000	3333	6667	F		20000	20000	0	
Special Grant	30000	15000	15000	F	1	30000	30000	0	
Donations	100	240	-140	U		500	1200	-700	U
Other	0	2000	-2000	U		1000	12000	-11000	U
Total Income	**48100**	**34573**	**13527**	**F**		**105500**	**147200**	**-41700**	**U**
EXPENDITURE									
Salaries	10000	12000	2000	F	2	66000	72000	6000	F
Temp Salaries	3000	500	-2500	U	2	7000	3000	-4000	U
Rent	1500	500	-1000	U		3000	3000	0	U
Gas	1000	300	-700	U		1600	1800	200	U
Electricity	1200	400	-800	U		2400	2400	0	U
Telephone	900	200	-700	U		2100	1200	-900	U
Provisions	5000	3000	-2000	U		28000	18000	-10000	U
Equipment Hire	800	500	-300	U		4800	3000	-1800	U
Maintenance	1000	200	-800	U		1000	1200	200	U
Cleaning	300	200	-100	U		1100	1200	100	U
Travel/Subsistence	300	100	-200	U		1200	600	-600	U
Expenses	500	100	-400	U		1400	600	-800	U
Laundry	200	200	0			1400	1200	-200	
Computers	0	5000	5000	F	3	0	10000	10000	F
Furniture	8000	5000	-3000	U	3	10000	10000	0	U
Major Repairs	7000	5000	-2000	U	3	11000	10000	-1000	U
Sundry	800	373	-427	U		1800	2000	200	U
Sub total	41500	33573	-7927	U		143800	141200	-2600	U
Central Services	2500	1000	-1500	U	4	12500	6000	-6500	U
Total Expenditure	**44000**	**34573**	**-9427**	**U**		**156300**	**147200**	**-9100**	**U**
Surplus/Deficit	**4100**	**0**				**-50800**	**0**		

KEY

VAR =	Variance
F =	Favourable
U =	Unfavourable
YTD =	Year to date

Explanatory Notes

1. Special grant should have been released in two stages, quarter 1 and quarter 2, however, the quarter 1 grant was received late.

2. There are two staff vacancies due to recruitment problems and agency staff have been used for cover.

3. These are areas of expenditure for which the special grant has been given.

4. Central services is a cost that is charged to the nursery school for support services such as finance and personnel supplied by the local authority.

Suggested solutions to this exercise can be found on page 141

PROJECTED OUTTURN ASSUMPTIONS

e) *Using the information in the previous part of this exercise, calculate the projected outturn for the year based on the following assumptions, and complete the pro-forma report on the next page.*

   a) *Spending on provisions will only be 50% of that in the first half of the year.*

   b) *Staff expenses will no longer be authorised.*

   c) *Computer will be purchased in the second half of the year, but a £1,000 virement will be made from this heading to compensate for the over spend on major repairs.*

   d) *All other headings have been assumed to continue at the same rate as in the first six months.*

Proforma Worksheet
To Calculate Projected Outturn

	YTD Actual	YTD Budget		Projected Outturn
INCOME				
Fees	54000	84000		
Revenue Grant	20000	20000		
Special Grant	30000	30000		
Donations	500	1200		
Other	1000	12000		
Total Income	**105500**	**147200**		
EXPENDITURE				
Salaries	66000	72000		
Temp Salaries	7000	3000		
Rent	3000	3000		
Gas	1600	1800		
Electricity	2400	2400		
Telephone	2100	1200		
Provisions	28000	18000	(a)	
Equipment Hire	4800	3000		
Maintenance	1000	1200		
Cleaning	1100	1200		
Travel/Subsistence	1200	600		
Expenses	1400	600	(b)	
Laundry	1400	1200		
Computers	0	10000	(c)	
Furniture	10000	10000		
Major Repairs	11000	10000		
Sundry	1800	2000		
Sub total	143800	141200		
Central Services	12500	6000		
Total Expenditure	**156300**	**147200**		
Overspend	**-50800**	**0**		

The projected outturn solution can be found on page 144

Exercise 11

Establishing Your Financial Management Information Needs

Complete the following questionnaire

1) What size of budget(s) has been (or will be) devolved to you?

   a) Up to £10,000 ☐
   b) £10,001 - £50,000 ☐
   c) £50,001 - £100,000 ☐
   d) £100,001 - £250,000 ☐
   e) Over £250,000 ☐

2) How many transactions do you expect during the year?

   a) Less than 4 ☐
   b) 5 to 10 ☐
   c) 11 to 25 ☐
   d) 26 to 100 ☐
   e) Over 100 ☐

3) How often do the transactions take place?

   a) Annually ☐
   b) Half yearly ☐

c) Monthly
d) Weekly
e) Daily

4) How simple is the budget(s) to control?

a) Very simple
b) Simple
c) Moderate
d) Quite difficult
e) Very difficult

5) What is the risk of overspending?

a) Very low
b) Low
c) Moderate
d) High
e) Very high

6) How easily can your main budget (the highest value) be profiled?

a) Very easily
b) Moderately
c) With some difficulty
d) With great difficulty

e) Cannot be profiled ☐

7) How would you describe the volatility of your main budget(s)?

a) Static ☐
b) Mildly fluctuating ☐
c) Moderately fluctuating ☐
d) Very volatile ☐
e) Totally unpredictable ☐

8) How do you rate the importance of the devolved budgets for which you are responsible, in relation to the total expenditure/performance of the organisation?

a) Not important ☐
b) Moderately important ☐
c) Important ☐
d) Very important ☐
e) A critical budget ☐

9) How do you rate your competency as a financial manager?

a) Very good ☐
b) Good ☐
c) Average ☐
d) Poor ☐
e) Very poor ☐

10) How seriously are devolved budgets being taken in your organisation?

a)	Not seriously	☐
b)	Quite seriously	☐
c)	Seriously	☐
d)	Very seriously	☐
e)	Budgetary control linked to performance related pay	☐

Suggested solutions to this exercise can be found on page 145

Exercise 12

Financial Management Information

Take a copy of a typical financial management report produced by your organisation:

✶ Consider how it measures up to the characteristics of good financial information:

*Is it **A**ccurate?*
*Is it **E**asy to understand?*
*Is it **I**nformative?*
*Is it **O**n time?*
*Is it **U**p to date?*

Summarise your findings

Chapter 6

Management and Financial Responsibility

Management Responsibility

In establishing a devolved budget, ideally financial and management responsibilities should be aligned. This means the person responsible for making management decisions about the service is also the person responsible for the budget. In the context of budgetary control, management responsibilities refer to those responsibilities relating to the day to day aspects of service delivery. A budget holder will therefore have management responsibilities if:

- *They have the ability to make decisions about resources used to deliver a service*
- *They have the ability to increase or decrease service levels (quantity and/or quality)*
- *They have the ability to influence the way in which the service is delivered (even if this is only controlling their own method of working)*

The following example illustrates the previous points:

A chef will have the day to day responsibility for food preparation, menus, and perhaps supervision of other catering staff. The budgets devolved to the chef would be those of food purchasing, and some aspects of the salary budget, such as overtime or temporary staffing.

The management responsibilities will involve deciding whether or not to purchase in bulk or to buy on a daily basis; the types of suppliers that are used; the content of the menus; and hence the types of food purchases to be made.

In some public sector organisations, the chef is divorced from such management decisions, and there may be a central purchasing unit that takes responsibility for all purchases and selects the approved suppliers. If this is the case, then it would be unfair to devolve such budgets to the chef because he/she has limited management responsibilities with respect to the service output, i.e. the meals prepared will be determined by the ingredients that have been made available.

The involvement of the budget holder in budget setting is very important to the management process, as the budget holder needs to be totally clear as to the outputs that are expected from the allocated budget. Even if the budget holder has had no involvement in the development of the budgets, they should be informed of the output/results that the devolved budget is expected to produce. If this information is not forthcoming, the budget holder has to develop a clear idea as to what can realistically be achieved with the budget and then create their own targets. For example, our chef should be aware of the number of meals that need to be provided with the catering budget, and any other objectives which have been set.

Financial Responsibility

A budget holder's financial responsibilities will include the following:

- *Checking that payments are only made for goods and services that have been received*
- *Authorising invoices for payment*
- *Coding payments to the correct account*
- *Checking that the actual transactions on each budget heading is correct*
- *Arranging for errors to be corrected*
- *Monitoring actual expenditure/income against budgets*

In order to meet their financial responsibilities, the budget holder should ideally have some involvement with the design format of the financial information being provided. This may mean liaising with an accountant or/an accounts department, or it may involve becoming familiar with the computerised financial systems where the budget holder has on-line access.

Most organisations operate some form of computerised accounting systems and depending on the organisation and the level of devolvement in place, budget holders may have different levels of access to online financial information. Levels of access may vary as follows:

No Access	⇨	Budget holders do not have direct access to online reports and only receive printed reports. Requests need to be made to the accounting department for other information.
Read Only Access	⇨	Budget holder has access to reports on a read only basis along with the ability to generate reports to be printed locally.
On line Access	⇨	Budget holder has an access level which enables them to effect transactions such as making payments and entering commitments as well as reviewing and generating reports.

In order to adequately discharge the budget holder's financial responsibilities, it is essential that a good working relationship is established with the providers of financial information, such as the accounts departments.

Linking Management and Financial Responsibilities

A key to successful devolved budgetary responsibility is ensuring financial and management responsibilities are aligned, as the two issues are linked. In introducing devolved budgetary responsibilities, some organisations have encountered very real problems by missing this essential point.

If the budget holder has management responsibility without financial responsibility, and wishes to make a management decision about the service which requires the use of the budget, then this may create problems. For example, the budget holder may have to go through a long process of obtaining authorisation, and in some cases may be told that the budget cannot be spent in a particular manner or has already been fully committed. This inhibits the way in which the service can be effectively delivered by slowing down the decision making process and creating inefficiencies generally.

If the budget holder has financial responsibility without management responsibility, budgetary control can again be very difficult. This is because other staff may make decisions about service delivery without the budget holder's knowledge. If overspending occurs, the budget holder will still be held accountable, even though the cause of the overspend was not as a result of their decision.

Accountability

An important element of successful devolved budgetary control is having an effective process for accountability. The budget holder will have no incentive to undertake the financial responsibilities if there is no method of accountability. Effective accountability can be achieved in several different ways.

- *Through the line manager system*
- *Through the performance appraisal system*

- *Through a service contract agreement*
- *Through the pay and benefits system*
- *Through the board/committee structures*

Each of the above approaches are discussed below:

Line Manager

Formal or informal reporting arrangements may exist to the line manager. The line manager will assess the budget holder's performance and will take the appropriate action. Hence, if the budget holder has not undertaken their duties to an adequate standard, the line manager could reprimand, admonish, or even recommend disciplinary action depending on the nature of the underperformance. Conversely, the line manager could praise the budget holder for successful budgetary control and perhaps recommend promotion or some kind of recognition, monetary or otherwise.

Performance appraisal

Many public sector organisations will have utilised some form of performance appraisal system. Such systems may or may not be linked to pay and benefits and/or promotion prospects. One feature of all performance appraisal systems is the need to assess the appraisee's performance against objectives, over a given timeframe. If budgetary control is a feature of the appraisee's duties, it should be assessed as part of the process. Poor performance in this area will result in low assessment scores.

Service Contract

Many sector bodies are requiring service providers to work under contract. In some cases, service contracts will arise as a result of contracting out public services, and in other instances internal service agreements are developed to generate greater efficiencies. These arrangements normally set targets for both service delivery and charges. The discipline of working within a contractual framework means that budget holders must keep within budget, otherwise the income generated from customers will not cover all the expenditure. In such arrangements the accountability is heightened, because any income shortfalls or overspending may result in reduced activity and perhaps redundancies. The managers of such services are accountable to their colleagues and customers for ensuring services and jobs are maintained.

Pay and benefits

Performance related pay schemes have been introduced in some areas of the public sector. Performance related pay can be structured such that budgetary control success is part of the formula for calculating pay and benefits. One example of this practice is where an organisation sets parameters for budget holders outlining that they must be within, say, 5% of their budget by the year end. If the budget holder failed to achieve these targets, then salary increments could be with-held, and in some cases a pay cut could be made. Conversely if the target was exceeded, i.e. savings where in excess of 5%, the budget holder may receive a bonus.

Boards/Committees

In some cases budget holders will be accountable to a board or a committee responsible for overall financial control of the organisation. In particular, budget holders who have overspent will be required to report the reasons to the board/committee, to which they will have to provide explanations for their financial position. These bodies may have the power to admonish and discipline if required.

The organisation which implements a devolved budgetary control system should also institute effective methods for accountability. Budget holders should be made aware as to how they are expected to account for their performance with regard to budgetary control.

Summary

- In order to ensure budget holders are given the best opportunity to effectively manage their budgets, it is important that management and financial responsibilities are aligned

- The involvement of budget holders in budget setting is crucial if they are to be clear about the outputs required. If this is not possible, budget holders should be thoroughly briefed about budgetary expectations

- There is a clear link between management and financial responsibility which if not recognised can create problems in budgetary control

- One of the keys to successful devolved budgetary control is having an effective process for accountability. This can be achieved through the line manager system, the appraisal system, service contracts, pay and benefits or boards/committees

Exercise 13

Being Responsible and Accountable

Scenario A

A training manager is responsible for arranging training courses during the year for a number of departments. Having established what each department requires she then organises the training on their behalf. She is not undertaking any direct delivery herself but is acting as the commissioner of training from external and internal sources. She has arranged for trainers to deliver courses on site; purchased some online tutorials and materials for internal training; and has organised inter departmental training where possible. She has negotiated that each department give her their training budgets to manage, in addition to a small centrally held budget. At the end of the year she will have to account both for service delivery and the amounts spent by department. At the moment, although invoices are received for the course materials, trainers, venues etc. and she keeps her own record, she is still unsure as to the real position. Her own records never seem to agree with the computer printouts she receives from the finance department.

At the end of the year she has overspent her own budget and when she totals the other departments budgets allocated to her, it is clear that there will also be an overspend of those budgets as well. In order to make the position look better she has been juggling the way in which expenditure has been coded against budgets, such that each budget will be only 1% overspent as opposed to some being over and some being under. A 1% overspend on training has been accepted by her line manager. When trying to negotiate for next year's programmes she is experiencing disgruntlement from some departments who now say they will not hand over their budgets to her. She does not understand what the problem is.

Scenario B

A legal services section of a local authority now has to charge all their time on a time recording system so as to adequately assess the cost of each area of work. This will allow the establishment of an internal trading account whereby each service is charged for the work undertaken. It has been accepted there is a need to have a central code for tasks undertaken directly on behalf of the organisation as a whole, as opposed to an individual department. There are some departments that require their services on a regular basis such as Social Services, Housing, Land and Properties, etc. and the Legal Services Manager considers he may be able to introduce a discount system for those departments, given the volume of work. Although time sheets have been completed there has not been a distinction between productive time and recoverable time to the client. In some cases it has been necessary to reduce the charge to clients if it is clear that more hours have been charged than should have been necessary for that particular job.

The Legal services also have to buy in certain services from outside, such as Counsel representation. At present there is no arrangement made as to how this cost is to be covered, and the Legal Services Manager had thought he could absorb this cost in the hourly rates. This has not been the case as Counsel's fees have been tremendous and have been charged to client departments directly, much to the annoyance of those departments who seem to think fees are high due to the poor performance of the Legal Services Department. The legal services manager has collected a lot of data from the time recording system, but still does not know how to charge clients and how to ensure the legal services costs are covered at the end of the year. This year there will be a budget overspend of 10%.

Consider the two scenarios given and decide in both cases:

a) who is responsible
b) who is accountable

for the budgets.

Suggested solutions to this exercise can be found on page 150

Exercise 14

How responsible and accountable are you?

- *Given the current climate within your organisation in relation to managing devolved budgets, do you consider that you are responsible and accountable for the budget(s) under your control?*

- *What incentives/penalties are currently in place to ensure budget holders take their responsibilities seriously?*

- *How do you consider your organisation could improve the way in which budget holders are made to be responsible and accountable for their devolved budgets?*

Chapter 7

Common Problems In Managing A Devolved Budget Answered

In this chapter we set out a number of typical problems that budget holders and managers may encounter in managing a devolved budget, and we suggest answers that may provide a practical way of solving these problems.

PROBLEM 1

I manage a budget but do not have the authority required to make the type of changes I would wish to make to the budget for the good of the service. For example, I cannot use salary budgets to fund other types of goods and services because salaries are ring fenced. Also I cannot change the grades of staff that I manage because the "establishment" is fixed, and the personnel department does not allow changes.

ANSWER 1

It is quite common for organisations to introduce elements of a devolved budgetary system on a stage by stage basis. In some cases this means the changes necessary for devolvement to work fully have not been made. Ideally, devolvement of budgets also means a devolvement of power to the budget holder, even though many senior managers may wish to retain certain powers. Every organisation should have "financial regulations" which identify roles and procedures regarding the conduct of their financial affairs. This may include restrictions such as ring fencing salary budgets. However, given the increasing pressure to ensure value for money in all public spending, it is advisable that budget holders have as much flexibility as possible.

Ideally, it is recommended that budget holders have the ability to make virements (transfers), between salary budgets and other budgets. If the budget holder is to adequately control the service, they should be able to create a staffing structure that matches the service even if this involves establishment changes. Any changes to staffing would have to be performed within the context of the organisation's personnel policies, and in some organisations this may take time to implement.

In order to work successfully within the current regime, the budget holder must clarify what can be done with savings made on salary budgets, i.e. can they be used to support overtime, or temporary staff payments, etc. This may provide some flexibility in the way in which staffing resources can be deployed. The best advice with respect to trying to achieve establishment changes is to lobby the organisation's key decision makers with proposals. Gaining senior management support is essential to align appropriate decision making power with budgetary responsibility.

PROBLEM 2

I consider myself to have good budgetary control skills, but I am frustrated in my efforts to manage my budget because half way through the year my budget is often cut without warning or explanation.

ANSWER 2

Central government has had a continuing policy to achieve efficiencies in public sector expenditure, and hence efficiency savings have been sought in all areas of public life including the police force, armed forces, local authorities, education and health authorities. Even if budgets are developed with extreme care, it is difficult to set a perfect budget. Consistent budget management throughout the year is the only way in which an organisation can aim to stay within budget by the year end. One action that may arise as a result of budgetary control activities is that budgets may need to be cut in some areas to account for overspending in others. Hence, budget holders who may have managed their budgets well during the year may experience cuts for the sake of the organisation as a whole, even though this may seem unfair.

The most frustrating aspect of the current process seems to be budget changes are made without warning and explanation. Budget holders may have to absorb cuts midway through the year which will affect all the existing plans for their service. The reasons for such change should always be explained with sufficient notice given.

In these cases, the budget holder when informed of the extent of the cuts needs to re-forecast the whole budget, revise the projected outturn on all budgets and then develop a new plan for the service. Budget reductions may result in certain service outputs planned at the beginning of the year not being met. Revisions to service delivery outputs and planned targets need to be made, and the relevant senior management informed of the impact of reducing budgets. If the budget holder takes this approach, senior management may in some cases reconsider the extent of the cuts, if the impact on services is shown to be detrimental or too severe.

> **PROBLEM 3**
>
> ***I have made every effort to be extremely prudent in my expenditure and have created a saving on my budget for the year. However, in my organisation, monies cannot be carried forward to the next year and any savings are used to balance other people's deficits. I wonder if there is any point in trying to save money if others are to benefit from it.***

ANSWER 3

Although the good of the whole organisation should come before that of an individual budget holder, some would suggest budget holders are more incentivised to make savings if they can utilise them within their own service area, as opposed to the savings being used elsewhere. To overcome this dissatisfaction there are a number of strategies that can be adopted:

Allow budget holders to keep a percentage of savings made	⇨	Allow, say, 50% of savings to be retained by the individual service area with the other 50% going to the general reserves or to fund deficits in other service areas.
Specific developments	⇨	Allow the individual service area achieving the savings to put forward their future plans for specific developments. These savings could then be utilised on projects that meet the organisation's priorities.
Trading Accounts	⇨	Allow each service area to operate an individual trading account. Surpluses and deficits will then be carried forward annually. Note: if surpluses are to be carried forward for the benefit of the service, then deficits would also be carried forward to the detriment of the service.
Recognition	⇨	Budget holders who make savings for the benefit of the organisation could be recognised for their efforts in some formal way, even though they are not allowed to keep savings achieved in their area.

PROBLEM 4

I struggle every month to control the budget because the financial management information I receive is very poor. It is out of date, often inaccurate, and very complex to understand. I am aware that it does not show how many invoices are waiting to be paid or my committed expenditure. The financial management report also only gives a cumulative position so I cannot see the individual month's transactions. The information never agrees with my manual records, therefore, I ignore the financial information I receive from the finance department in favour of my spreadsheet figures.

ANSWER 4

Keeping one's own records may help to counter poor financial management information. However, a reconciliation between one's own records and the organisation's financial management information is essential.

Reconciling the manual records to a computerised system, which may be lagging behind, can be time consuming. However, with the aid of a spreadsheet, reconciliations can be performed in a straight forward manner as follows:

Step 1	List actual figures appearing on the financial report produced by the main accounting system
Step 2	List actual figures as calculated by your locally kept records. These will include commitments and creditors (outstanding bills)
Step 3	Calculate the difference between the two figures. These figures represent the differences that require reconciliation
Step 4	Identify the reason for the difference in each case. These will often be timing differences with respect to creditors and commitments. However, they may also be due to error.
Step 5	No action needed if the differences are due to timing. If they are due to error, further work needs to be done to identify how the error has occurred, and then corrective action taken. This may involve making an adjustment to the main accounting system.

Keeping separate records is useful if the quality of the financial information from the main accounting system is not AEIOU, (see chapter 5). If local records are being well maintained and relied upon, it is advisable to use these actual figures when undertaking budget monitoring and control procedures.

PROBLEM 5

I have given up trying to control my budget because I do not have the time, I do not have any clerical back up or assistants, and I do not even have access to a computer.

ANSWER 5

If the organisation has a strategy of devolved budgetary control, and really believes that this is the most efficient way to control budgets, then budget management must be given some priority. Devolvement of budgets requires the budget holder to have additional duties over and above the main focus of their jobs, and an allowance needs to be made for this with respect to the allocation of resources. Ideally resources should be devolved along with the budgetary responsibility. In some organisations, this has been achieved by devolving central finance officers to departments to assist managers with their budgetary responsibilities.

To undertake the role properly, time needs to be allocated to monitoring and managing budgets. In order to achieve this, one of two things must happen - either the budget holder has to put in additional time (overtime paid or unpaid), or some of the existing duties have to lapse in favour of budget management, or both. The organisation will need to advise budget holders of its priorities so that managers can be effective with regards to their own personal time management.

Devolving budgetary control requires investment in people (training and additional administrative support) and resources (usually technological). If this is not forthcoming then compromises in workloads will have to be made.

PROBLEM 6
At this organisation there has been no financial training or preparation for being a budget holder. No wonder we have all failed miserably and have overspent again as usual.

ANSWER 6

When an organisation devolves budgets, and particularly where a great many staff become budget holders, financial training is essential. Due to the technical nature of this training, it may be an area that cannot be delivered by the in-house training department (if one exists). Occasionally the organisation looks to the finance department to provide the training. The difficulty with this approach comes if there is no individual within the department with trainer skills, or who wishes to develop those skills. The other problem is identifying personnel who will have time to set aside to deliver training programmes. It is for these reasons why some organisations provide insufficient finance training for budget holders.

Timing of the training is also important. Some organisations invest a great deal of resources in finance training before devolved budgets are implemented, only to find that devolvement does not take place until considerably later. By then those who attended the training require refresher courses, and there may be new employees who did not attend the initial training. This would highlight the need to have a continuous rolling programme of training, pitched at a number of levels, to meet the different skills and abilities of budget holders.

There are external courses run from time to time, particularly by representative bodies of the sector, and by professional institutes and associations to which public sector employees may belong. For example, courses are sometimes delivered by some public sector unions for the benefit of members and non-members.

It is possible to obtain training aids, books, etc. to help budget holders with their self-development. Although there are many products on the market, most are focused on private sector finance and not easily transferable to the public sector. The books in this series provide excellent material to assist budget holders improve their skills.

PROBLEM 7

I have never been asked about setting the budget although I am expected to control the budget. I don't know where any of the figures came from, and they do not relate to the way in which the service is currently being run. For example, some budgets we never use, and other areas are essential but have no budgets allocated to them.

ANSWER 7

The key to effective budgetary control is having a well thought out budget to begin with. It is ideally the role of the budget holder to be closely involved in budget preparation. In so doing, the budget holder is clear about all the assumptions behind each of the budget headings, and how the budgets relate to the way in which the service is to be delivered (including the objectives and targets that should be met during the year).

In some cases it is not practical for the budget holder to prepare the budgets. However, there should always be a certain level of consultation. Even if this is not the case, as stated in the question, the budget holder can still be proactive about how the budget can be used to correctly reflect the service objectives. This can be achieved by following the P.A.T.H.:

Prepare assumptions that make sense for the current service

Ask for headings and budgets to be changed as required

Take positive action to get changes implemented

Have confidence to redefine the budget within cash limits

When the budget has been redefined to meet service requirements, the assumptions should be well documented. This allows any new budget holder to understand how the budget has been formulated. This approach will require a lot of initial work at the beginning of the year, but will make budgetary control for the rest of the year far easier.

PROBLEM 8

I am always told that savings are needed at the beginning of each financial year, but somehow in the last month of the year, I am always being requested to spend all this money that has suddenly appeared from nowhere. I know that I often waste the money but I'm told I either spend it, or lose it in next year's budget allocation.

ANSWER 8

This problem arises from the same reasons stated in the answer to problem 3. If it is possible to carry forward underspends into a following year, there would be no need to spend up to the limit of the budget each year. If the policy of carrying forward monies from one year to the next is not in place, this situation can easily occur. To avoid this happening on a large scale, budgets should be profiled across the year. If they are correctly profiled, underspending can be identified far earlier and appropriate corrective action taken. Ideally, if there are areas where underspends are going to arise, the additional resources that become available should be spent effectively, in a planned way throughout the year, and not rushed in the last month.

In addition to having budgets profiled, the other effective tool to quickly identify underspends, is to regularly calculate the projected outturn figure either monthly or quarterly. This figure will show if the projected end of year expenditure is below the estimated budget for the year. This allows revision to expenditure plans to take place at an early stage.

> ***PROBLEM 9***
> ***How can I control budgets that are uncontrollable? I have to respond to need, just like a fireman I can't let the house burn down because the budget is insufficient to pay staff overtime. As for having to generate an income target - I can't possibly predict how many people are going to buy our information booklets.***

ANSWER 9

There is no doubt that budgets of a demand led nature are more difficult to monitor and control than budgets for controllable service areas. However, an uncontrollable budget will still require close management.

Managing a demand led budget ideally requires criteria by which the level of need is determined. This should be monitored closely such that the service meets the defined need in the most appropriate and cost effective manner.

It is also advisable to have an expenditure plan based on clear assumptions about the expected level of need. This estimate may not be correct because in a demand led service it may be difficult to predict the demand accurately. However, this approach will allow budget holders to regularly monitor the differences between actual and estimated demand. Very high deviations from the initial estimates will mean there is likely to be over or under spends.

In the case of likely overspends, the impact on the budget should be estimated. Any shortfalls should then be brought to the attention of senior management, who may either have to seek additional funds, or take other appropriate action, such as changing the need criteria, or reducing spending on other services.

Estimating demand in a needs led service may be undertaken by looking at historic trends and trying to establish patterns that can be projected into the future. For example, the fire service should be able to estimate the average number of call outs per week based on historic experience. The service should also be able to estimate the number of call outs that require no action; the number of those that require extensive resources to be deployed; the geographical location more prone to fires; and which times of year fires are more likely to occur. Even though each year will be different, there will be a data bank of information that will help to identify whether or not the demand for the service will be very different (higher or lower) from one month to the next, and from one year to another. This data can then be fed into the budgetary control system, and budgets adjusted accordingly.

Income arising from sales, fees, charges, etc., is also demand led, and can be difficult to predict and control. For example, local authority leisure centres and planning departments are often hit with large fluctuations in income, often related to seasonal and economic factors. In addition, unlike the private sector, many public services that generate income may face restrictions from central government, or other bodies such as pricing regulators. This means that they may not be able to control price levels, and therefore cannot make price adjustments to compensate for demand fluctuations.

A budget holder with an income target will need to ensure the target is realistic to begin with, taking into account the current market conditions. The budget holder will also need to identify some way of monitoring the factors that affect demand. In some cases, a marketing strategy should be developed to promote the service and generate more customers.

PROBLEM 10
I am a public servant and not an accountant. I refuse to be held accountable for budgets - its not my job!

ANSWER 10

This is a feeling that has been echoed by many in public service; doctors, head teachers, social workers, civil servants, planners, police, armed forces and so on, have all been met with budget constraints and stricter accountability. The fact is the role of a public servant has evolved over the years, and now includes an element of financial management and control, as well as other aspects of management and service delivery. Most new comers to the public sector are well aware of the importance of achieving value for money, and the fact that everyone has to play a role in ensuring budgets are spent as effectively as possible. For some public servants, whose job descriptions did not include this role, there has been a change in culture to which they have had to adjust.

If change is imposed quickly, many people tend to be left behind and feel resentful when it comes to undertaking new duties. The answer is to ensure that everyone participates, and can see the relevance to their individual roles in the changing organisation. If possible, change should be viewed positively as an opportunity to take a fresh look at things and develop new skills, new techniques, and ultimately better services.

Solutions to Exercises

Solutions to Exercises

Solution to Exercise 1

Devolvement in Practice

(a) To assist with this solution an organisational chart showing the various levels of responsibility is shown on the next page. Budgets can be split by service area, e.g. Entertainment, and then by activity, e.g. Catering, and then by type, e.g. Food. The number of budget heads will vary depending on the nature and complexity of each service area. Management and financial responsibilities should be aligned. Therefore, whoever is responsible for ordering cleaning materials should have the budget for this spend; in this case the cleaning services manager (or could even be devolved to a lower grade if practical). Similarly the catering manager would have the food purchases budget. These officers are at 4th tier grades in the organisational chart overleaf. Salaries on the other hand, may be devolved to head of service or held at a higher level in order to maximise flexibility and control.

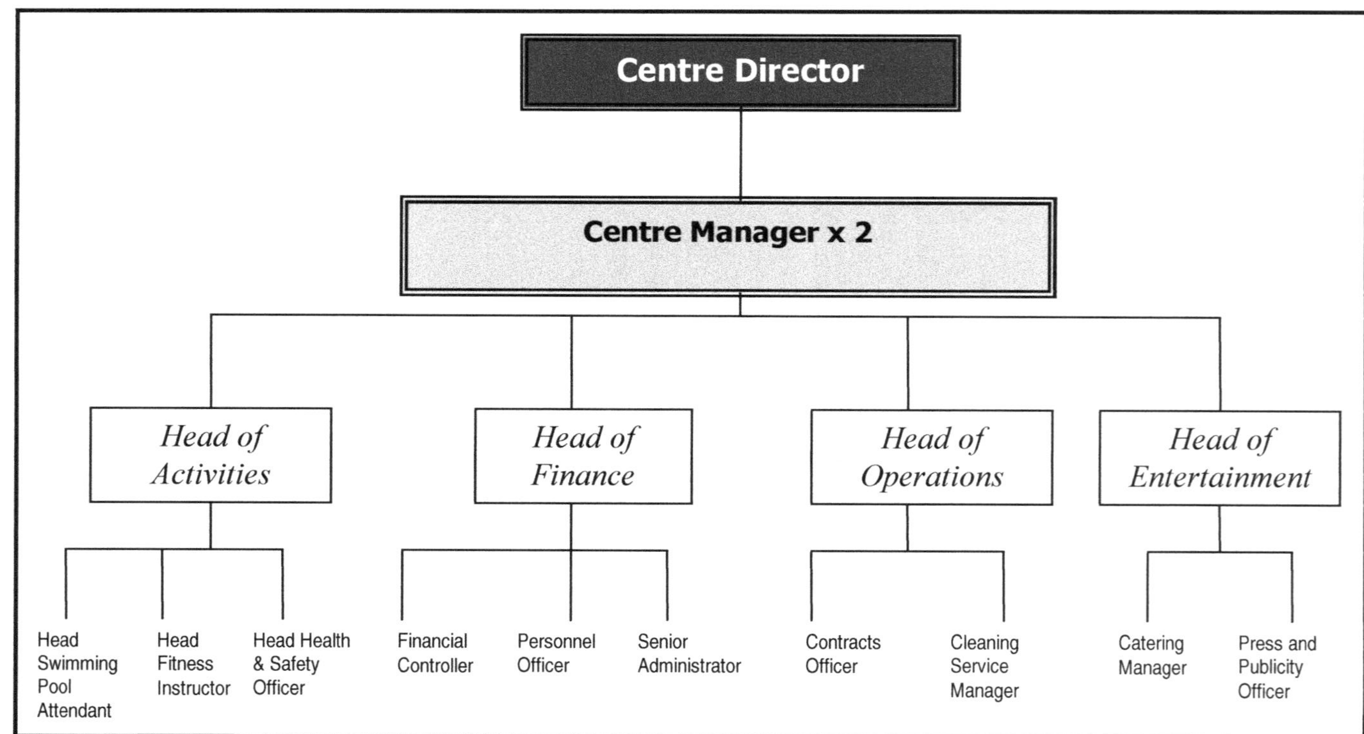
Centre Director
Centre Manager x 2
Head of Activities
Head of Finance
Head of Operations
Head of Entertainment
Head Swimming Pool Attendant
Head Fitness Instructor
Head Health & Safety Officer
Financial Controller
Personnel Officer
Senior Administrator
Contracts Officer
Cleaning Service Manager
Catering Manager
Press and Publicity Officer

(b) Problems may include:

* *Size of budget (i.e. if it is too large to be effectively managed or too small to warrant devolvement due to impracticalities)*

* *Complex nature of accounting and reporting*

* *Ability of staff to manage budgets*

* *Increased levels of administration due to the need for increased monitoring and control*

* *Dis-economies of scale*

Solutions may include:

* *Good financial systems which allows for adequate coding and management reports*

* *Training for all staff with budgets*

* *Clear management reporting lines and levels of authority*

* *Regular supervision and review*

* *Continuous independent review of budgets by the head of finance to ensure budgets are devolved where there is a practical benefit, and not just for the sake of devolvement*

Solution to Exercise 3

Developing a Budget from First Principles

a) Action points should include:

* *Identifying demand and service level*
* *Identifying key objectives of the service*
* *Clarifying the quality criteria required*
* *Identifying how the service is to be delivered e.g. organisational structure, physical resource requirements etc.*
* *Identifying how the activity will be funded e.g. public contributions, 100% subsidy or less, grants, fees, charges, etc.*

b) Typical areas will include salaries, overhead items such as rent, electricity, etc. Sources of information will vary depending on the structure and type of organisation selected. However, it should include written estimates, personnel departments, published data etc., comparisons with other similar organisations, historical information where available.

c) There is no perfect answer as a number of issues can be debated, however, there should be consistency between the easiest and the most difficult. The difficult areas to budget for are those that will depend on income from the public and are totally demand led such as the leisure centre, as opposed to those that are providing an in-house service such as a personnel department which has relatively fixed budgetary requirements.

An example of a possible ranking is given as follows:

Area	Rank	Reasoning
Quality Assurance Division	1	Fixed service not dependent on volume or selling services
Contracts Management Unit	2	As above, but may depend on the number of contracts to be managed each year.
An Advice Centre	3	As above, but may depend on the number of users
Personnel Department	4	May have a range of services, some of which may have to be "sold", e.g. training places
Meals on Wheels	5	Depending on how it is delivered, if under contract may be subject to varying demands on a daily basis
Secondary School	6	State schools receive formula funding depending on pupil intake number each year which may vary. Private schools depend on fees per pupil and are subject to varying demand and changes throughout the year
Fire Brigade	7	Due to the nature of the service, volumes cannot be predicted, but service has to be delivered on demand regardless of budget implications
Hospital	8	Similar to above with added complexity if income depends on a number of private beds being sold
Residential Nursing Home	9	On the assumptions that all places have to be sold on the open market without a block contract, there could be a totally variable income throughout the year
Leisure Centre	10	As above but there is an added complexity given the wide range of activities and services being provided, and the wide ranging pricing policy which is normally required

Solution to Exercise 4

Incremental Budgeting

BUDGET WORKING PAPERS

Employee Costs

Name	Basic Pay	Pay Award (note 1)	Total	Nat. Ins.	Pension	Budget
J Brown	40,000	600	40,600	4,243	2,436	47,279
A Taylor	30,000	563	30,563	3,194	1,834	35,591
P Pritkash	22,000	413	22,413	2,342	1,345	26,100
C Doyle	20,000	375	20,375	2,129	1,223	23,727
O Obayo	18,000	203	18,203	1,902	1,092	21,197
D Lincoln	15,000	169	15,169	1,585	910	17,664
R Cohen	13,200	149	13,349	1,395	801	15,545
TOTAL						**187,103**

Operational Costs

	Costs Last Year		Inflation		Budget
Transport Costs	10,000		300		10,300
Premises Costs	50,000		1,500		51,500
Supplies and Services	80,000		2,400		82,400
New Developments	0				13,500
Financing Costs	10,000		100		10,100
TOTAL					**167,800**
TOTAL BUDGET					**354,903**

Note 1: Pay award has only a 9 month effect because it begins on 1st July (i.e. award calculated as 9/12ths)

Solution to Exercise 5
Profiling Budgets

PROFILED BUDGET													
	Apr	May	Jun	Jul	Aug	Sep	Oct	Nov	Dec	Jan	Feb	Mar	Total
INCOME													
Fees	75,000	75,000	75,000	75,000	75,000	75,000	75,000	75,000	75,000	75,000	75,000	75,000	900,000
Total	75,000	75,000	75,000	75,000	75,000	75,000	75,000	75,000	75,000	75,000	75,000	75,000	900,000
EXPENDITURE													
Salaries	40,000	40,000	40,000	40,800	40,800	37,740	37,740	37,740	37,740	37,740	37,740	37,740	465,780
Central Recharges			20,000			20,000			20,000			20,000	80,000
Supplies and Services	5,000	5,000	5,000	5,000	5,000	5,000	5,000	5,000	5,000	5,000	5,000	5,000	60,000
Transport Costs	750	750	750	750	750	750	2,250	2,250	2,250	2,250	2,250	2,250	18,000
Professional Fees	10,000	10,000	10,000	10,000	10,000	10,000	10,000	10,000	10,000	10,000	10,000	10,000	120,000
Contingency	5,575	5,575	7,575	5,655	5,655	7,349	5,499	5,499	7,499	5,499	5,499	7,499	74,378
TOTAL	61,325	61,325	83,325	62,205	62,205	80,839	60,489	60,489	82,489	60,489	60,489	82,489	818,158
Surplus/Deficit Month	*13,675*	*13,675*	*-8,325*	*12,795*	*12,795*	*-5,839*	*14,511*	*14,511*	*-7489*	*14,511*	*14,511*	*-7,489*	*81,842*

Salaries: April to June (£480,000/12 = £40,000 per month), July to August £40,000 per month plus 2% = £40,800), September to March £40,800 minus {£36,000 plus 2% divided by 12} £3,060 = £37,740.
Transport: April to September £18,000 x 25% divided by 6, October to March £18,000 x 75% divided by 6. **Contingency:** 10% of all expenditure

Solution to Exercise 7
Variance Analysis

1. Interpretation of variances

a) Overspend of £200 occurring in month 6 assuming previous periods on target

b) On target

c) Overspend averaging £200 per month over the last 6 months

d) Compensating savings made in month 6 to correct previous overspends, cumulative position still in overspend

e) Overspend in month 6 of £400 reducing previous brought forward underspends resulting in a cumulative overspend of £200

f) On target for the month but an historic overspend which must have occurred in previous months

g) Underspend of £200 occurring in month 6 assuming previous periods on target

Information affecting interpretation will include:

- Profile of budget
- Staff numbers and salary levels
- Definition of "salaries" i.e. what is included in this figure
- Activity levels *

* *e.g. (b) appears to be on target but if the budget had been based on 3 employees being in post and only 2 are currently in post, then (b) is not on target as one would have expected an underspend on the budget. Variances must be interpreted with supporting management information.*

2. Example causes of variances may be:

- Seasonality
- Changes in levels of activity compared to planned activity
- Poor profiling
- Long term sickness
- Inefficiency

3. Examples of uncontrollable variances may be:

- Demands for statutory services
- Changes in legislation e.g. implementation of new health and safety procedures
- Central recharges and allocations

4. Examples of key control mechanisms may be:

- Freeze/reduce expenditure by setting a limit
- Reduce the level of service being provided e.g. opening hours
- Increase income by charging more for services or introducing a charge

- Identify underspent budgets to mitigate overspent ones (virement)

Solution to Exercise 8

Role of the Budget Holder

a) Steps to be taken from the beginning of the year:

Budget needs to be allocated to each floor/division based on an assessment of need. This should be achieved by initially researching the existing position and establishing furniture requirements for the coming year. Monitoring can then be undertaken on a floor by floor basis.

b) Systems will include:

- Ordering system
- Authorisation process
- Appropriate coding systems such that reports may be generated
- Validation process such that goods received are checked to invoices
- Furniture register/log so that volumes can be monitored
- Preferred supplier lists to enable choice
- Accounting system that generates variance analysis
- Complaints procedure if people are not satisfied

c) Some steps to reduce complaints will include:

- Negotiation and compromise will have to take place in order for the cash limited budget to be divided fairly on a basis of need and for each division to be made aware of their individual budget for furniture. This will enable each area to maintain their own record of purchases if necessary.

- Continued updates should be given to inform divisions of the status of the furniture budget relating to their area

- The budget allocation should be reviewed on a regular basis to take account of any changes to the current position of each division

Solution to Exercise 10

Understanding Financial Management Information

a) The initial reaction should be concern regarding the scale of unfavourable variances However, to arrive at a true assessment of the situation, the additional information requested should include:

1. *Basis of the budget (budget assumptions)*
2. *The total budget for the whole year*
3. *The profiles that have been used*
4. *The occupancy rates within the school*
5. *The level of fees being charged*
6. *The level of outstanding fees to be collected*
7. *The strategy to raise donations*
8. *The make up of the other income and strategy to achieve budget*
9. *What is happening with respect to the recruitment of full time staff?*
10. *Who are the temporary staff and are they in fact covering the vacant posts*
11. *Current stock levels of the provisions*

12. *Details of menus being provided*

13. *List of equipment being hired*

14. *Nature of travel and subsistence and staff expenses*

15. *Plans for purchasing the computer*

16. *Confirmation that all major repairs are completed*

b) Short term actions, largely based upon assumptions made, should include:

- *Revising budgets for the second half year based on projected activity to the end of the year; i.e. calculating the projected outturn*

- *Requesting and receiving the additional information highlighted*

- *Specific changes to some aspects such as the food purchases, telephone, expenses, the way in which fees are collected, recruitment etc. Stricter control and authorisation procedures should be instituted*

- *Finance training for the manager and staff*

Long term actions, based upon assumptions made, should include:

- *Implementation of a marketing strategy if occupancy is a problem*

* *Implementation of a strict credit control policy if fee collection is a problem*

* *Review of the school in terms of its long term viability*

* *Consideration of closure, alternative uses etc.*

c) Key management techniques include:

* *Communication with all members of staff*

* *Include staff in the decision making process with respect to the formulation of actions to address the position*

* *Devolve/delegate certain budgets to staff so that they are more aware of what is available to spend, e.g. give the catering manager the food budget*

* *Institute regular reporting mechanisms such that management information is provided on a regular basis*

* *Institute closer supervision*

* *Set targets for performance*

d) Key monitoring techniques

* *Review of financial management information on a regular basis*

* *Review of other management reports such as occupancy and debtors*

* *Regular meetings and progress reports*
* *Regular review of targets against actual performance*

e)

	YTD Actual	YTD Budget	Projected Outturn
INCOME			
Fees	54000	84000	108,000
Revenue Grant	20000	20000	40,000
Special Grant*	30000	30000	30,000
Donations	500	1200	1,000
Other	1000	12000	2,000
Total Income	**105500**	**147200**	**181,000**
EXPENDITURE			
Salaries	66000	72000	132,000
Temp Salaries	7000	3000	14,000
Rent	3000	3000	6,000
Gas	1600	1800	3,200
Electricity	2400	2400	4,800
Telephone	2100	1200	4,200
Provisions**	28000	18000	42,000
Equipment Hire	4800	3000	9,600
Maintenance	1000	1200	2,000
Cleaning	1100	1200	2,200
Travel/Subsistence	1200	600	2,400
Expenses***	1400	600	1,400
Laundry	1400	1200	2,800
Computers****	0	10000	9,000
Furniture	10000	10000	10,000
Major Repairs	11000	10000	11,000
Sundry	1800	2000	3,600
Sub total	143800	141200	260,200
Central Services	12500	6000	25,000
Total Expenditure	**156300**	**147200**	285,000
Overspend	-50800	0	-104,200

* Assume special grant is one off and will not continue

** 2nd half 50% of £28,000 = £14,000 add to 1st half £28,000 = £42,000

*** Expenses no longer authorised so total equals spend in 1st half

**** Balance of special grant after £10,000 for furniture and £11,000 for major repairs deducted

All other headings double the YTD actual

Solution to Exercise 11

Establishing your Financial Management Information Needs

Score the answers given as follows:

(a) 5 (b) 4 (c) 3 (d) 2 (e) 1

Total your combined scores for questions 1 to 10 then read the appropriate summary of your financial information requirements. You may find it useful to evaluate each budget separately if you are responsible for a number of different budgets.

10 - 23

This score would indicate that the budget holder should have a high dependency for comprehensive financial management information. This should include the following:

1. At least monthly, if not weekly financial management reports which show variances for the discrete period and the cumulative period. Variances should be stated both in actual terms and percentage terms. If the system used is a cash accounting system, then a list of all commitments (unpaid invoices and orders raised) will also be required and details of accrued expenditure where relevant

2. A monthly revision of the projected outturn based on the most current circumstances and a review of future spending activity for the rest of the year

3. An exception report which highlights major variances and gives detailed explanations of the cause of each variance

4. Access to detailed transactions listings when required

5. On line access to a computerised financial information system

6. An activity report showing levels of service, this may be a time analysis of hours spent, occupancy rates, customer contact time etc.

7. If a staff related budget is one of the areas under the budget holder's control, then reports will be required on employee numbers, pay rates, sickness levels, salary enhancements, expense claims, time sheets and so on

8. If income is an area of responsibility then a break down of income sources will be required along with debtors' listings etc.

You may be receiving some of this information if not all of it. However, if any of this information is not being received, you have a financial information requirement.

24 - 37

The budget holder with this score is in a position of requiring regular information which is relatively detailed. The information requirement is not quite as comprehensive as the budget holder that has scored 10 to 23, however, the key reports would include the following:

1. Monthly financial management reports which show variances for the discrete period and the cumulative period. Variances should be stated both in actual terms and percentage terms. If the system used is a cash accounting system, then a list of all commitments (unpaid invoices and orders raised) will also be required and details of accrued expenditure where relevant

2. A monthly revision of the projected outturn based on the most current known circumstances and a review of future spending activity for the rest of the year

3. On line access to a computerised financial information system

4. An activity report showing levels of service, this may be a time analysis of hours spent, occupancy rates, customer contact time etc.

5. If a staff related budget is one of the areas under the budget holder's control, then reports will be required on employee numbers, pay rates, sickness

levels, salary enhancements, expense claims, time sheets and so on

6. If income is an area of responsibility then a break down of income sources will be required along with debtors listings etc.

You may be receiving some of this information if not all of it. However, if any of this information is not being received you have a financial information requirement.

38 - 50

The Budget holder with this score is in the fortunate position of having budgets that are reasonably stable and easy to control, however, they should not be complacent. Even the most straight forward budget still requires monitoring and may sometimes not go according to plan. The financial information required for these budgets include the following:

1. Monthly financial management reports which show variances for the discrete period and the cumulative period. Variances should be stated both in actual terms and percentage terms. If the system used is a cash accounting system, then a list of all commitments (unpaid invoices and orders raised) will also be required and details of accrued expenditure where relevant

2. A quarterly revision of the projected outturn based on the most current known circumstances and a review of future spending activity for the rest of the year

3. Occasional activity reports

4. If a staff related budget is one of the areas under the budget holder's control, then reports will be required on employee numbers, pay rates, sickness levels, salary enhancements, expense claims, time sheets and so on.

5. If income is an area of responsibility then a break down of income sources will be required along with debtors listings etc.

You may be receiving some of this information if not all of it. However, if any of this information is not being received you have a financial information requirement.

Solution to Exercise 13

Being Responsible and Accountable

Scenario A

- Training manager responsible and accountable for her own budget
- Other departments responsible and accountable for the budgets delegated to the training manager
- Training manager accountable to the departments

The reason the departments remain responsible and accountable for the budgets given to the training manager, is that she was only acting as an intermediary on their behalf. This means the departments should have been ensuring that they were aware of the status of these budgets at all times and should have taken corrective action when it was clear that they were beginning to become out of control.

Scenario B

- The legal services manager is responsible and accountable for the legal services expenditure budget, and the income budget arising from charges to clients
- As the decision making with respect to instructing Counsel remains in the legal services department, it would be appropriate that this budget is also the responsibility of the legal services manager. However, there may be an argument that the Legal Services manager cannot be accountable for these fees as they are outside of his direct control

INDEX

A

B

C

D

E

F

H

I

L

M

N

O

P

Q

R

S

T

U

V

W

Z

For further information see www.hbpublications.com
and www.fci-system.com

www.ingramcontent.com/pod-product-compliance
Ingram Content Group UK Ltd.
Pitfield, Milton Keynes, MK11 3LW, UK
UKHW020129250726
13967UKWH00002B/557

9 781899 448722